defining breaking dawn

Vocabulary Workbook for Unlocking the *SAT, ACT®, GED®, and SSAT®

Brian Leaf, M.A.

WILEY

Wiley Publishing, Inc.

Library of Congress Cataloging-in-Publication Data:
Leaf, Brian.
 Defining Breaking dawn : vocabulary workbook for unlocking the SAT, ACT, GED, and SSAT / Brian Leaf.
  p. cm.
 ISBN 978-0-470-63999-3 (pbk)
 ISBN 978-0-470-90125-0 (ebk)
 1. Vocabulary tests--Study guides. 2. Vocabulary--Study and teaching (Secondary). 3. Educational tests and measurements--Study guides. 4. Meyer, Stephenie, 1973- Breaking dawn. I. Title. II. Title: Vocabulary workbook for unlocking the SAT, ACT, GED, and SSAT.
 PE1449.L313 2010
 428.1'076--dc22
               2010029175
Printed in the United States of America

10 9 8 7 6 5 4 3 2 1

Book production by Wiley Publishing, Inc., Composition Services

Acknowledgments

Thanks to Stephenie Meyer for her storytelling and her terrific vocabulary. Thanks to my agent, Linda Roghaar, and my fantastic editors at Wiley, Greg Tubach and Carol Pogoni. Thanks to Amy Sell and Adrienne Fontaine at Wiley for getting the word out. Thanks to Pam Weber-Leaf for great editing tips, Zach Nelson for sage marketing advice, Ian Curtis for assiduous proofreading, Manny and Susan Leaf for everything, and of course, thanks most of all to Gwen, Noah, and Benjamin for love, support, and inspiration.

Table of Contents

About the Author

Brian Leaf, M.A., is the author of *Defining Twilight, Defining New Moon, Defining Eclipse,* and the four-book SAT and ACT test-prep series *McGraw-Hill's Top 50 Skills for a Top Score.* He is Director of the New Leaf Learning Center in Massachusetts, and has provided SAT, ACT, GED, SSAT, and GRE preparation to thousands of students throughout the United States. Brian also works with the Georgetown University Office of Undergraduate Admissions as an alumni interviewer, and is a certified yoga instructor and avid meditator. For more information, visit his Web site at www.brianleaf.com.

How to Use This Book

This workbook contains 40 groups of vocabulary words selected from *Breaking Dawn.* Many of these words will show up on your SAT, ACT, GED, or SSAT. Beginning at Group 1, refer to the *Breaking Dawn* page where each vocabulary word appears. Read the word in context and come up with a definition. Then check your definitions against those provided in this workbook and make corrections. I'll also show you synonyms, word parts, and memorization tools. Read these over a few times, and then complete the drills. Do that for all 40 groups. There's no easier or more fun way to learn 600 vocabulary words! By the end of this book, your vocabulary will be larger, your test scores will be higher, and you'll be a *Breaking Dawn* scholar!

Inevitable Revelation

Find each of the following words on the *Breaking Dawn* page number provided. Based on the way each word is used in the book, guess at its definition.

1. **Inevitable** (p. 1) might mean _____

   _____

2. **Reverence** (p. 6) might mean _____

   _____

3. **Staid** (p. 6) might mean _____

   _____

4. **Resigned** (p. 10) might mean _____

   _____

5. **Omniscient** (p. 11) might mean _____

   _____

6. **Tenuous** (p. 12) might mean _____

   _____

7. **Ominous** (p. 13) might mean _____

   _____

8. **Revelation** (p. 14) might mean _____

   _____

Let's see how you did. Check your answers, write the exact definitions, and reread the sentence in *Breaking Dawn* where each word appears. Then complete the drills on the next page.

1. **Inevitable** (p. 1) means *unavoidable.* I love the *preface* (introductory chapter) in each of the *Twilight* books in which you get a brief glimpse of what's to come in the book. Interestingly, three of the four books in the *Twilight* saga use the word *inevitable* or the related words *inexorable* (unstoppable), *relentless* (persistent), or *impending* (looming) in the preface or first chapter! Synonym: ineludible.

2. **Reverence** (p. 6) means *deep respect.* Any car lover would treat Bella's Mercedes Guardian with respect. Too bad Jake's not around; he'd surely enjoy it. *Reverence* is easy to remember; it sounds likes *Reverend* (a minister), a person for whom most people show **deep respect.**

3. **Staid** (p. 6) means *dull and unadventurous.* I remember this word because it sounds like *stay,* as in *stay at home*—be unadventurous. Synonyms: decorous (proper), sedate, sober, somber.

4. **Resigned** (p. 10) means *accepting defeat or some other undesirable result,* almost like **resigning** from a job that's too difficult. To Charlie, Billy seems to have given up, to have **resigned** himself to the fact that Jake has run away. Charlie has good intentions, but Billy knows that Jake needs time to heal.

5. **Omniscient** (p. 11) means *knowing everything. Omni-* means *all,* as in *omnipresent* (present **all** over) and *omnipotent* (**all**-powerful), and *-scient* refers to *knowing,* as in *science* (the gathering of knowledge). So *omniscient* means *all-knowing—knowing everything.*

6. **Tenuous** (p. 12) means *weak* or *flimsy.*

7. **Ominous** (p. 13) means *threatening.* Synonyms: foreboding, inauspicious, menacing. SAT, ACT, GED, and SSAT reading comprehension passages always include a few questions about the tone of a passage. *Tone* is expressed through an author's choice of words and punctuation. You can see the *ominous* (threatening) tone of this page from words like "fidgeting," "murder," "rattled," "horror," "victim," and "flinched." Bella is expecting an ugly scene when she and Edward tell Charlie about the good news; she even wants Edward to wait until after Charlie has put away his gun!

8. **Revelation** (p. 14) means *surprising or dramatic announcement or realization.*

Synonyms: Select the word or phrase whose meaning is closest to the word in capital letters.

1. INEVITABLE
   - A. inexorable
   - B. decorous
   - C. sedate
   - D. sober
   - E. somber

2. REVERENCE
   - A. omnipresence
   - B. omniscience
   - C. deep respect
   - D. thankfulness
   - E. peace

3. STAID
   - A. relentless
   - B. impending
   - C. ineludible
   - D. resigned
   - E. sedate

4. OMNISCIENT
   - A. knowing nothing
   - B. knowing something
   - C. knowing everything
   - D. knowing most things
   - E. knowing nobody

Analogies: Select the answer choice that best completes the meaning of the sentence.

5. Ominous is to menacing as
   - A. tenuous is to strong
   - B. inauspicious is to foreboding
   - C. threatening is to resigned
   - D. reverent is to disrespectful
   - E. omniscient is to decorous

6. Inevitable is to certain as
   - A. impending is to unlikely
   - B. ineludible is to sure
   - C. omnipresent is to resigned
   - D. staid is to tenuous
   - E. ominous is to definite

Sentence Completions: Choose the word that, when inserted in the sentence, <u>best</u> fits the meaning of the sentence as a whole.

7. Homer had a _____; he realized that he loved his family and must save his town.
   - A. reverence
   - B. resignation
   - C. nap
   - D. donut
   - E. revelation

8. Hoping to capture the _____ tone of the scene, Manuel used dark and threatening words to write the chapter.
   - A. tenuous
   - B. ineludible
   - C. ominous
   - D. inexorable
   - E. decorous

1. **A.** *Inevitable* means *unavoidable. Inexorable* means *unstoppable* and is the best answer choice. *Decorous, sedate, sober,* and *somber* mean *dull and unadventurous.*

2. **C.** *Reverence* means *deep respect.* Use the process of elimination—cross out all choices that are **definitely** wrong. *Omnipresence* means *present all over,* and *omniscience* means *all-knowingness.*

3. **E.** *Staid* and *sedate* mean *dull and unadventurous. Relentless, impending,* and *ineludible* mean *unavoidable. Impending* also implies that something is *about to happen. Resigned* means *given up.*

4. **C.** *Omniscient* means *knowing everything.*

5. **B.** Make a sentence with the two words. For example, "Ominous means the same thing as menacing." Then, try your sentence for each pair of words in the answer choices.

   A. Tenuous (flimsy) means the same thing as strong . . . no.
   B. Inauspicious (threatening) means the same thing as foreboding (threatening) . . . yes!
   C. Threatening means the same thing as resigned (given up) . . . no.
   D. Reverent (deeply respectful) means the same thing as disrespectful . . . no.
   E. Omniscient (all-knowing) means the same thing as decorous (proper) . . . no.

6. **B.** "Inevitable means certain to happen."

   A. Impending (about to happen) means unlikely to happen . . . no.
   B. Ineludible (unavoidable) means sure to happen . . . yes.
   C. Omnipresent (present all over) means resigned (given up) to happen . . . no.
   D. Staid (dull and unadventurous) means tenuous (flimsy) to happen . . . no.
   E. Ominous (threatening) means definite to happen . . . no.

7. **E.** Think of a word to fill the blank. Often you can borrow a word right out of the sentence.

   "Homer had a _realization_; he realized that he loved his family and must save his town."

   Base your answer **only** on evidence in the question. The sentence always describes the word needed to fill the blank. You know that Homer (of *The Simpsons*) loves naps and donuts, but the sentence gives evidence **only** that he had a realization. *Revelation* means *dramatic realization.*

8. **C.** "Hoping to capture the _threatening_ tone of the scene, Manuel used dark and threatening words to write the chapter."
   When trying to come up with a word to fill the blank, always look for evidence in the sentence—you want a word that means "dark and threatening." *Ominous* means *threatening.*

Unforeseen Guffaws

Find each of the following words on the *Breaking Dawn* page number provided. Based on the way each word is used in the book, guess at its definition.

1. **Serene** (p. 14) might mean _____

_____

2. **Fleetingly** (p. 15) might mean _____

_____

3. **Guffaws** (p. 17) might mean _____

_____

4. **Foreseen** (p. 17) might mean _____

_____

5. **Nuptials** (p. 19) might mean _____

_____

6. **Trilling** (p. 20) might mean _____

_____

7. **Debonair** (p. 20) might mean _____

_____

8. **Futilely** (p. 21) might mean _____

_____

6 Let's see how you did. Check your answers, write the exact definitions, and reread the sentence in *Breaking Dawn* where each word appears. Then complete the drills on the next page.

Definitions

1. **Serene** (p. 14) means *calm and peaceful.* Synonyms: equanimous, poised (calm and composed), tranquil.

2. **Fleetingly** (p. 15) means *temporarily.* Let's play *Name That Movie!* See if you can name the movie that contains this quote: "Summer romances end for all kinds of reasons. But when all is said and done, they have one thing in common: They are shooting stars . . . a spectacular moment of light in the heavens, a **fleeting** glimpse of eternity. And in a flash, they're gone." (Check your answer in the Quiz and Review Solutions.) Synonyms for *fleeting*: ephemeral, evanescent, impermanent, transient.

3. **Guffaws** (p. 17) means *loud, hearty laughs.*

4. **Foreseen** (p. 17) means *predicted.* That makes sense since *fore-* means *in front,* as in *foreshadow* (warn in advance). So *foreseen* means *seen in front—predicted.* Synonym: presaged.

5. **Nuptials** (p. 19) means *wedding.*

6. **Trilling** (p. 20) means *soft and vibrating,* like the song of a sparrow. Synonyms: crooning, quavering, warbling.

7. **Debonair** (p. 20) means *stylish and charming,* and comes from the French phrase *de bon air,* meaning *of good disposition.* Synonyms: genteel, suave, urbane.

8. **Futilely** (p. 21) means *uselessly* or *pointlessly.* Synonym: in vain.

Synonyms: Select the word or phrase whose meaning is closest to the word in capital letters.

1. SERENE
   A. guffawing
   B. trilling
   C. equanimous
   D. genteel
   E. urbane

2. FLEETING
   A. ephemeral
   B. futile
   C. in vain
   D. poised
   E. tranquil

3. FORESEEN
   A. evanescent
   B. impermanent
   C. transient
   D. debonair
   E. presaged

4. FUTILE
   A. trilling
   B. in vain
   C. quavering
   D. warbling
   E. inexorable

Analogies: Select the answer choice that best completes the meaning of the sentence.

5. Fleeting is to time as
   A. serene is to calm
   B. guffaw is to laughter
   C. tenuous is to strength
   D. debonair is to style
   E. omniscient is to knowledge

6. Debonair is to sloppy as
   A. genteel is to ineludible
   B. urbane is to resigned
   C. foreseen is to presaged
   D. equanimous is to agitated
   E. fleeting is to transient

Sentence Completions: Choose the word that, when inserted in the sentence, best fits the meaning of the sentence as a whole.

7. John and his fiancée eagerly prepared for their _____; they wrote their own vows, chose the location, and selected the bridal party.
   A. nuptials
   B. tranquility
   C. evanescence
   D. revelation
   E. resignation

8. Sam had not foreseen how _____ he would feel wearing a tux to the party; on the contrary, he had imagined that it would make him feel tense and clumsy.
   A. ephemeral
   B. urbane
   C. futile
   D. vain
   E. relentless

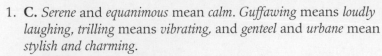

1. **C.** *Serene* and *equanimous* mean *calm*. *Guffawing* means *loudly laughing*, *trilling* means *vibrating*, and *genteel* and *urbane* mean *stylish and charming*.

2. **A.** *Fleeting* and *ephemeral* mean *temporary*. *Futile* and *in vain* mean *useless*, and *poised* and *tranquil* mean *calm*.

3. **E.** *Foreseen* and *presaged* mean *predicted*. *Evanescent, impermanent*, and *transient* mean *temporary*. *Debonair* means *stylish and charming*.

4. **B.** *Futile* and *in vain* mean *useless*. *Trilling, quavering*, and *warbling* mean *vibrating*. *Inexorable* means *unstoppable*.

5. **C.** "Fleeting means very little time."
   A. Serene (calm) means very little calm . . . no.
   B. Guffaw (laugh loudly) means very little laughter . . . no.
   C. Tenuous (weak) means very little strength . . . yes.
   D. Debonair (stylish and charming) means very little style . . . no.
   E. Omniscient (all-knowing) means very little knowledge . . . no.
   If your sentence was "Fleeting is related to time," then all of the choices would work. If that happens, make your sentence more specific. Try to define the first word using the second word, such as "Fleeting means very little time."

6. **D.** "Debonair (stylish and charming) is the opposite of sloppy."
   A. Genteel (stylish and charming) is the opposite of ineludible (unavoidable) . . . no.
   B. Urbane (stylish and charming) is the opposite of resigned (given up) . . . no.
   C. Foreseen (predicted) is the opposite of presaged (predicted) . . . no.
   D. Equanimous (calm) is the opposite of agitated . . . yes.
   E. Fleeting (temporary) is the opposite of transient (temporary) . . . no.

7. **A.** Think of a word to fill the blank, selecting a word directly from the sentence when possible, and then see which answer choice fits best.

   "John and his fiancée eagerly prepared for their *vows/ wedding*; they wrote their own vows, chose the location, and selected the bridal party."

   Nuptials means *wedding* and fits best.

8. **B.** "Sam had not foreseen how *relaxed and not clumsy* he would feel wearing a tux to the party; on the contrary, he had imagined that it would make him feel tense and clumsy."
   Use the process of elimination—cross out answer choices that are **definitely** wrong, and choose the best of what's left. *Urbane* means *stylish and charming* and fits best.

Spectacle

Find each of the following words on the *Breaking Dawn* page number provided. Based on the way each word is used in the book, guess at its definition.

1. **Spectacle** (p. 22) might mean _____

   _____

2. **Qualms** (p. 27) might mean _____

   _____

3. **Blasé** (p. 29) might mean _____

   _____

4. **Medium** (p. 30) might mean _____

   _____

5. **Cavalier** (p. 30) might mean _____

   _____

6. **Horde** (p. 31) might mean _____

   _____

7. **Defection** (p. 31) might mean _____

   _____

8. **Fathom** (p. 34) might mean _____

   _____

Let's see how you did. Check your answers, write the exact definitions, and reread the sentence in *Breaking Dawn* where each word appears. Then complete the drills on the next page.

1. **Spectacle** (p. 22) means *something interesting to look at.* In fact, *spect-* means *look* as in *inspect* (look at—*examine*), *spectacles* (eyeglasses), and *circumspect* (*circum-* means *around,* so *look around—be cautious*). Learning word parts is a terrific way to improve your vocabulary— you have a much better chance of understanding a new word that contains any of the word parts that you're learning in this book.

2. **Qualms** (p. 27) means *doubts.* Synonyms: misgivings, reservations.

3. **Blasé** (p. 29) means *casual or bored.* Synonyms: apathetic, cavalier, dismissive, indifferent, insouciant, nonchalant, offhand, perfunctory, phlegmatic (calm and casual). Standardized tests love to use these words; I'd say that at least one appears on every SAT!

4. **Medium** (p. 30) means *canvas, vehicle,* or *instrument.* "Jasper's medium was moods" means that Jasper's special gift works on people's moods; they are his **canvas,** and he can paint them however he pleases.

5. **Cavalier** (p. 30) means *casual* or even *casual to the point of being disrespectful,* and was a synonym for *blasé. Blasé* implies *a bored or* **disinterested** *casualness,* whereas *cavalier* implies *a* **disrespectful** *casualness,* like when Juno tells her best friend Leah, "I'm telling you I'm pregnant, and you're acting shockingly cavalier." (*Juno,* Fox Searchlight Pictures, 2007)

6. **Horde** (p. 31) means *mob.*

7. **Defection** (p. 31) means *abandonment.* Synonyms: apostasy, desertion, perfidy (disloyalty).

8. **Fathom** (p. 34) in this case means *understand.* It can also mean *measure the depth of,* like when *Glee*'s Sue Sylvester says to Finn and Rachel, "That copy machine is for Cheerios use only, paid for by alumni donations. I can't begin to **fathom** the damage you'd have done to the program, had you broken it." (*Glee,* "Showmance," FOX, 2009)

Synonyms: Select the word or phrase whose meaning is closest to the 11 word in capital letters.

1. BLASÉ
   A. circumspect
   B. apathetic
   C. ominous
   D. foreboding
   E. inauspicious

3. HORDE
   A. mob
   B. medium
   C. qualm
   D. misgiving
   E. reservation

2. CAVALIER
   A. debonair
   B. stylish and charming
   C. genteel
   D. urbane
   E. overly casual

4. FATHOM
   A. love
   B. hate
   C. understand
   D. regret
   E. mislead

Analogies: Select the answer choice that best completes the meaning of the sentence.

5. Blasé is to insouciant as
   A. dismissive is to ephemeral
   B. indifferent is to apathetic
   C. nonchalant is to evanescent
   D. cavalier is to transient
   E. perfunctory is to futile

6. Circumspect is to careless as
   A. indifferent is to reverent
   B. staid is to wild
   C. decorous is to tenuous
   D. sedate is to ominous
   E. somber is to inauspicious

Sentence Completions: Choose the word or words that, when inserted in the sentence, best fits the meaning of the sentence as a whole.

7. Natalia was mesmerized by the _____; she had never seen something so fascinating.
   A. medium
   B. horde
   C. furtive
   D. qualms
   E. spectacle

8. Samantha was angry with Philip for leaving their team to join the opposing _____, and took weeks to forgive his _____.
   A. mob .. nuptials
   B. group .. reverence
   C. medium .. perfidy
   D. horde .. defection
   E. guffaws .. desertion

1. **B.** *Blasé* and *apathetic* mean *casual*. *Circumspect* means *cautious;* and *ominous, foreboding,* and *inauspicious* mean *threatening*.

2. **E.** *Cavalier* means *overly casual*. *Debonair, genteel,* and *urbane* mean *stylish and charming*.

3. **A.** *Horde* means *mob*. *Medium* means *canvas, vehicle,* or *instrument*. *Qualm, misgiving,* and *reservation* mean *doubt*.

4. **C.** *Fathom* means *understand*.

5. **B.** "Blasé (casual) means the same thing as insouciant (casual)."
   - A. Dismissive (casual) means the same thing as ephemeral (temporary) . . . no.
   - (B.) Indifferent (casual) means the same thing as apathetic (casual) . . . yes.
   - C. Nonchalant (casual) means the same thing as evanescent (temporary) . . . no.
   - D. Cavalier (overly casual) means the same thing as transient (temporary) . . . no.
   - E. Perfunctory (casual) means the same thing as futile (useless) . . . no.

6. **B.** "Circumspect (cautious) is the opposite of careless."
   - A. Indifferent (casual) is the opposite of reverent (respectful) . . . maybe.
   - (B.) Staid (dull and unadventurous) is the opposite of wild . . . yes.
   - C. Decorous (proper) is the opposite of tenuous (weak) . . . no.
   - D. Sedate (unadventurous) is the opposite of ominous (threatening) . . . no.
   - E. Somber (unadventurous) is the opposite of inauspicious (threatening) . . . no.

   The words in choice B are more directly opposite than the words in choice A. *Casual* is not necessarily the opposite of *respectful,* whereas *unadventurous* is definitely the opposite of *wild.* Make sure to try all of the choices; don't stop with the first one that seems to work.

7. **E.** "Natalia was mesmerized by the *something fascinating;* she had never seen something so fascinating."

   You want a word for *something fascinating*. Use the process of elimination. *Spectacle* means *something interesting to look at* and fits best.

8. **D.** "Samantha was angry with Philip for leaving their team to join the opposing *team*, and took weeks to forgive his *leaving*."

   Think of a word to fill each blank and use the process of elimination for one blank and then the other. Only cross out choices that **definitely** do not fit—if a word might work in the blank or if you're not sure of a word's meaning, do not cross it off. *Horde* means *mob,* and *defection* means *abandonment*.

Group 4
Commended

Find each of the following words on the *Breaking Dawn* page number provided. Based on the way each word is used in the book, guess at its definition.

1. **Legion** (p. 34) might mean _____

   _____

2. **Inquisitive** (p. 35) might mean _____

   _____

3. **Disposition** (p. 35) might mean _____

   _____

4. **Furtively** (p. 39) might mean _____

   _____

5. **Reproach** (p. 40) might mean _____

   _____

6. **Aversion** (p. 40) might mean _____

   _____

7. **Cavernous** (p. 41) might mean _____

   _____

8. **Commendation** (p. 43) might mean _____

   _____

Let's see how you did. Check your answers, write the exact definitions, and reread the sentence in *Breaking Dawn* where each word appears. Then complete the drills on the next page.

Definitions

1. **Legion** (p. 34) means *association of lots of people or things,* or vampires in this case. Synonym: host.

2. **Inquisitive** (p. 35) looks like *inquire* (ask) and means *curious.*

3. **Disposition** (p. 35) means *way of being* or *character.* So, Aro's "inquisitive disposition" refers to his *curious way of being.* He loves to gather knowledge—I suppose anyone who has lived for 3,000+ years needs a hobby. Synonyms: constitution, temperament.

4. **Furtively** (p. 39) means *secretively and nervously.* Charlie glances **secretly and nervously** toward his fishing gear because he's edgy and wishes he were fishing instead of getting dressed up in a tuxedo. Synonyms: clandestinely, covertly, surreptitiously.

5. **Reproach** (p. 40) means *scolding.* Synonyms: admonishment, castigation, censure, excoriation, obloquy, rebuke, reprimand, reproof, vituperation. Standardized tests like to use the phrase *above reproach,* which means *above or beyond scolding—without fault, perfect.*

6. **Aversion** (p. 40) means *strong dislike.* It can also mean *avoidance,* which makes sense since one might **avoid** things that one **strongly dislikes.** The SAT, ACT, GED, and SSAT love to use a word with several meanings and ask you to determine its meaning in the context. Synonyms: animosity, antipathy, disinclination, enmity.

7. **Cavernous** (p. 41) means *very spacious,* like a big cavern. Synonyms: capacious, voluminous.

8. **Commendation** (p. 43) means *praise.* Synonyms: acclaim, accolade, appreciation, esteem, homage, kudos, plaudits, tribute. Let's play *Name That Movie!* In what recent film did Kirk Lazarus (Robert Downey, Jr.) say to Tugg Speedman (Ben Stiller), "That's the stuff that **accolades** are made of"? Hint: In the same movie, Tom Cruise stole the show with his hilarious dance to Ludacris' song "Get Back." Check your answer in the Quiz and Review Solutions.

Synonyms: Select the word or phrase whose meaning is closest to the word in capital letters.

1. FURTIVE
   A. clandestine
   B. inquisitive
   C. cavalier
   D. perfunctory
   E. phlegmatic

2. REPROACH
   A. aversion
   B. animosity
   C. reproof
   D. disinclination
   E. enmity

3. CAVERNOUS
   A. voluminous
   B. covert
   C. surreptitious
   D. trilling
   E. warbling

4. COMMENDATION
   A. good deeds
   B. plaudits
   C. censure
   D. rebuke
   E. reprimand

Analogies: Select the answer choice that best completes the meaning of the sentence.

5. Reproach is to accolades as
   A. admonishment is to animosity
   B. censure is to antipathy
   C. rebuke is to kudos
   D. antipathy is to defection
   E. enmity is to reservations

6. Kindness is to disposition as
   A. legion is to host
   B. covert is to look
   C. attitude is to cavalier
   D. fathom is to understand
   E. qualm is to doubt

Sentence Completions: Choose the word or words that, when inserted in the sentence, <u>best</u> fits the meaning of the sentence as a whole.

7. Harry did not want Katie to see him watching her, but his _____ nature got the best of him, so he glanced _____ at her while they passed in the hall.
   A. curious .. cavernously
   B. phlegmatic .. surreptitiously
   C. insouciant .. covertly
   D. menacing .. reverently
   E. inquisitive .. furtively

8. Arin realized that he had a _____ of options and that each of these many choices could solve his dilemma.
   A. host
   B. disposition
   C. constitution
   D. temperament
   E. spectacle

Solutions

1. **A.** *Furtive* and *clandestine* mean *secret*. *Inquisitive* means *curious*. *Cavalier* means *overly casual*, *perfunctory* means *casual*, and *phlegmatic* means *calm and casual*.

2. **C.** *Reproach* and *reproof* mean *scolding*. *Aversion*, *animosity*, *disinclination*, and *enmity* mean *dislike*.

3. **A.** *Cavernous* and *voluminous* mean *very spacious*. *Covert* and *surreptitious* mean *secret*, and *trilling* and *warbling* mean *vibrating*.

4. **B.** *Commendation* and *plaudits* mean *praise*. Make sure you try all of the choices. Don't just get to an answer that reminds you of the word and stop. *Good deeds* (choice A) deserve praise, but *plaudits* (choice B) means *praise*, so choice B is the best answer. Always try all choices and use the process of elimination to find the *best* answer. Notice that *plaudits* looks a lot like *applause*, and both mean *praise*.

5. **C.** "Reproach (scolding) is the opposite of accolades (praise)."
   - A. Admonishment (scolding) is the opposite of animosity (dislike) . . . no.
   - B. Censure (scolding) is the opposite of antipathy (dislike) . . . no.
   - (C.) Rebuke (scolding) is the opposite of kudos (praise) . . . yes.
   - D. Antipathy (dislike) is the opposite of defection (abandonment) . . . no.
   - E. Enmity (dislike) is the opposite of reservations (doubts) . . . no.

6. **B.** "Kindness is a type of disposition (way of being)."
   - A. Legion (large group) is a type of host (large group) . . . no, they mean the same thing.
   - (B.) Covert (secret) is a type of look . . . yes.
   - C. Attitude is a type of cavalier (overly casual) . . . no, the reverse: *cavalier* is *a type of attitude*.
   - D. Fathom (understand) is a type of understand . . . no, they mean the same thing.
   - E. Qualm (doubt) is a type of doubt . . . no, they mean the same thing.

7. **E.** "Harry did not want Katie to see him watching her, but his *????* nature got the best of him, so he glanced *????* at her while they passed in the hall."

   If you can't come up with a word to fill a blank, try the choices, and base your answer on evidence in the sentence. You have no evidence that Harry was *phlegmatic* (calm and casual) or *insouciant* (casual or bored), only that he was curious to watch her. *Inquisitive* means *curious*, and *furtively* means *secretly*.

8. **A.** "Arin realized that he had a *bunch* of options and that each of these many choices could solve his dilemma."

   Host means *large group* and works best.

Lots of Gossamer

Find each of the following words on the *Breaking Dawn* page number provided. Based on the way each word is used in the book, guess at its definition.

1. **Gossamer** (p. 48) might mean _____

   _____

2. **Catalyst** (p. 52) might mean _____

   _____

3. **Manfully** (p. 55) might mean _____

   _____

4. **Negligence** (p. 56) might mean _____

   _____

5. **Quarantined** (p. 68) might mean _____

   _____

6. **Flagellate** (p. 69) might mean _____

   _____

7. **Trepidation** (p. 75) might mean _____

   _____

8. **Sultry** (p. 81) might mean _____

   _____

18 Let's see how you did. Check your answers, write the exact definitions, and reread the sentence in *Breaking Dawn* where each word appears. Then complete the drills on the next page.

1. **Gossamer** (p. 48) means *delicate* and also refers to *the thin and very delicate cobwebs spun by small spiders*. Synonyms: diaphanous, sheer, wispy.

2. **Catalyst** (p. 52) means *motivator*. The magic Bella refers to in this passage is, of course, the ability to turn into a wolf. And the **catalyst** she refers to is the Cullens' move back into town. The Cullens came when Jacob was the right age, but if they had arrived twenty years earlier, Billy would have been the *alpha* (head) wolf! Synonyms: impetus, precipitant, stimulus.

3. **Manfully** (p. 55) means *with determination or bravery*. Synonyms: boldly, gallantly, intrepidly, pluckily, resolutely, valiantly.

4. **Negligence** (p. 56) looks like *neglect* (lack of proper care) and means *carelessness*.

5. **Quarantined** (p. 68) means *isolated to prevent injury or spread of disease to others*. You hear this term occasionally on medical shows such as *Scrubs* and *House, M.D.*

6. **Flagellate** (p. 69) means *whip*. You might recognize this word from biology class. *Protozoa* (microscopic organisms) use **flagella** to swim around. The flagella **whip** around and push the organism along. If you're not sure of the meaning of a word on a test, ask yourself whether you've seen or heard the word in a class, in a movie, or in a song. That might be enough to determine the meaning of a word and determine whether it's the correct answer to a question.

7. **Trepidation** (p. 75) means *fear*. Synonyms: angst, foreboding.

8. **Sultry** (p. 81) means *hot and humid*. You can get this from the context. They are on a tropical island, it's hot out, the air is salty, and they are on the beach. Interestingly, this word can also mean *passionate* or *sensual* as in a **sultry** dance. That's a nice double meaning as Bella and Edward begin their honeymoon together!

Synonyms: Select the word or phrase whose meaning is closest to the word in capital letters.

1. GOSSAMER
   A. manful
   B. gallant
   C. intrepid
   D. diaphanous
   E. valiant

2. CATALYST
   A. impetus
   B. acclaim
   C. esteem
   D. homage
   E. tribute

3. TREPIDATION
   A. negligence
   B. foreboding
   C. constitution
   D. temperament
   E. perfidy

4. SULTRY
   A. terrified
   B. stylish and charming
   C. hot and humid
   D. rude and calm
   E. tall and lean

Analogies: Select the answer choice that best completes the meaning of the sentence.

5. Intrepid is to trepidation as
   A. sultry is to guffaws
   B. resolute is to nuptials
   C. plucky is to futility
   D. circumspect is to qualms
   E. equanimous is to agitation

6. Plucky is to valiant as
   A. sheer is to wispy
   B. capacious is to clandestine
   C. voluminous is to covert
   D. inevitable is to staid
   E. inexorable is to decorous

Sentence Completions: Choose the word that, when inserted in the sentence, <u>best</u> fits the meaning of the sentence as a whole.

7. Heidi _____ herself for ignoring Brian's emails and wished that she could apologize for the offense.
   A. quarantined
   B. commended
   C. trilled
   D. revered
   E. flagellated

8. Lila was always eager for a challenge and never let fear stop her, so her friends called her Lila the _____.
   A. negligent
   B. quarantined
   C. intrepid
   D. foreboding
   E. catalyst

1. **D.** *Gossamer* and *diaphanous* mean *delicate*. Remember to use the process of elimination—cross off answers that **definitely** don't work and choose the best of what's left. *Manful, gallant, intrepid,* and *valiant* mean *brave*.

2. **A.** *Catalyst* and *impetus* mean *motivator*. *Acclaim, esteem, homage,* and *tribute* mean *praise*.

3. **B.** *Trepidation* and *foreboding* mean *fear*. *Negligence* means *lack of care, constitution* and *temperament* mean *way of being,* and *perfidy* means *disloyalty* or *abandonment*.

4. **C.** *Sultry* means *hot and humid*.

5. **E.** "An intrepid (brave) person does not have trepidation (fear)." *In-* means *not,* so *intrepid* means *not trepid—not fearful—brave*.
   - A. A sultry (hot and humid) person does not have guffaws (loud laughs) . . . no.
   - B. A resolute (brave) person does not have nuptials (a wedding) . . . no.
   - C. A plucky (brave) person does not have futility (uselessness) . . . no.
   - D. A circumspect (cautious) person does not have qualms (doubts) . . . no.
   - (E.) An equanimous (calm) person does not have agitation . . . yes.

6. **A.** "Plucky (brave) means the same thing as valiant (brave)."
   - (A.) Sheer (delicate) means the same thing as wispy (delicate) . . . yes.
   - B. Capacious (spacious) means the same thing as clandestine (secret) . . . no.
   - C. Voluminous (spacious) means the same thing as covert (secret) . . . no.
   - D. Inevitable (unavoidable) means the same thing as staid (dull and unadventurous) . . . no.
   - E. Inexorable (unstoppable) means the same thing as decorous (proper) . . . no.

7. **E.** "Heidi *apologized* herself for ignoring Brian's emails and wished that she could apologize for the offense."
   Flagellate means *whip* and fits best. Choose the answer that best fits the evidence in the sentence. You have no evidence that Heidi *quarantined* (isolated), *commended* (praised), *trilled* (vibrated), or *revered* (deeply respected) herself for ignoring Brian's emails, only that she wanted to **apologize** for the offense. *Flagellate* (whip) seems a bit strong, but is the only choice that fits the evidence.

8. **C.** "Lila was always eager for a challenge and never let fear stop her, so her friends called her Lila the *not stopped by fear*."
   Intrepid means *brave*.

Quiz 1

I. Let's review some of the words that you've seen in Groups 1–5. Match each of the following words to the correct definition or synonym on the right. Then check the solutions on page 171.

1.	Inevitable	A.	Decorous
2.	Staid	B.	Equanimous
3.	Ominous	C.	Urbane
4.	Serene	D.	Ineludible
5.	Fleeting	E.	Insouciant
6.	Debonair	F.	Menacing
7.	Qualms	G.	Ephemeral
8.	Cavalier	H.	Clandestine
9.	Defection	I.	Gallantly
10.	Disposition	J.	Perfidy
11.	Furtive	K.	Reservations
12.	Reproach	L.	Temperament
13.	Catalyst	M.	Fear
14.	Manfully	N.	Motivator
15.	Trepidation	O.	Admonishment

II. Let's review several of the word parts that you've seen in Groups 1–5. Match each of the following word parts to the correct definition or synonym on the right. Then check the solutions on page 171.

16.	Omni-	A.	Look
17.	Scient-	B.	Not
18.	Spect-	C.	Around
19.	Fore-	D.	Knowing
20.	Circum-	E.	All
21.	In-	F.	In front

Uncondtional Love

Find each of the following words on the *Breaking Dawn* page number provided. Based on the way each word is used in the book, guess at its definition.

1. **Implicitly** (p. 83) might mean _____

   _____

2. **Unconditionally** (p. 83) might mean _____

   _____

3. **Pallid** (p. 84) might mean _____

   _____

4. **Prosaic** (p. 86) might mean _____

   _____

5. **Deluge** (p. 86) might mean _____

   _____

6. **Taut** (p. 87) might mean _____

   _____

7. **Corresponding** (p. 87) might mean _____

   _____

8. **Angst** (p. 91) might mean _____

   _____

Let's see how you did. Check your answers, write the exact definitions, and reread the sentence in *Breaking Dawn* where each word appears. Then complete the drills on the next page.

1. **Implicitly** (p. 83) in this case means *completely,* but can also mean *implied.* Bella describes this word later in the sentence: One might trust a partner *implicitly* (completely) when there is **absolute** (complete) commitment. Synonym: unconditionally.

2. **Unconditionally** (p. 83) means *completely—without conditions.* Bella has just found the suitcase of French *sheer* (thin) lace lingerie that Alice packed for her and is wondering what to wear to the beach to meet Edward. She's afraid, but the *unconditional* (complete) love that they share for each other gives her courage. Synonyms: consummately, unequivocally, unqualifiedly.

3. **Pallid** (p. 84) means *pale.* Synonyms: ashen, blanched, sallow, wan.

4. **Prosaic** (p. 86) means *ordinary and unimaginative* and comes from the word *prose,* which refers to *ordinary writing,* as opposed to *poetry,* which has a less **ordinary** structure and is often more **imaginative.** Synonyms: conventional, pedestrian.

5. **Deluge** (p. 86) means *flood.* Synonyms: cascade, cataract, inundation, spate, torrent.

6. **Taut** (p. 87) means *tight or tense.*

7. **Corresponding** (p. 87) means *similar* or *matching.* This is an interesting word to break apart. *Cor-* means *together,* so *corresponding* means *responding together—fitting together or matching,* "proof that I belonged with him." Synonyms: analogous, commensurate, equivalent, homologous, proportional.

8. **Angst** (p. 91) means *anxiety* and was a synonym for *trepidation* in Group 5. Synonym: disquietude.

Synonyms: Select the word or phrase whose meaning is closest to the word in capital letters.

1. UNCONDITIONAL
   A. unequivocal
   B. unsuspecting
   C. unbelievable
   D. unappreciated
   E. unapproved

2. PALLID
   A. implicit
   B. taut
   C. corresponding
   D. sallow
   E. homologous

3. PROSAIC
   A. analogous
   B. pedestrian
   C. commensurate
   D. equivalent
   E. proportional

4. DELUGE
   A. angst
   B. trepidation
   C. disquietude
   D. enmity
   E. inundation

Analogies: Select the answer choice that best completes the meaning of the sentence.

5. Prosaic is to staid as
   A. conventional is to ashen
   B. pedestrian is to somber
   C. negligent is to taut
   D. intrepid is to implicit
   E. urbane is to corresponding

6. Serene is to disquiet as
   A. commensurate is to gossamer
   B. equivalent is to apathetic
   C. homologous is to surreptitious
   D. consummate is to partial
   E. intrepid is to plucky

Sentence Completions: Choose the word or words that, when inserted in the sentence, <u>best</u> fits the meaning of the sentence as a whole.

7. If the reservoir overflows, it will equally effect everyone who lives nearby; residents of both the city and the country can expect _____ of approximately _____ size.
   A. floods .. futile
   B. inundations .. analogous
   C. quarantines .. cavernous
   D. catalysts .. legion
   E. cascades .. reverential

8. Noka firmly believed that Ben should be admitted into the Honors Program, so he wrote a strong letter of recommendation praising Ben _____.
   A. tautly
   B. unconditionally
   C. proportionally
   D. valiantly
   E. cavalierly

1. **A.** *Unconditional* and *unequivocal* mean *complete*.
2. **D.** *Pallid* and *sallow* mean *pale*. *Implicit* means *complete*, *taut* means *tight*, and *corresponding* and *homologous* mean *matching*. You might recognize the word *homologous* from biology class; **homologous** chromosomes form a **matching** pair during *meiosis* (cell division). And that makes me think of the biology class scene in *Twilight* when Bella and Edward first met!
3. **B.** *Prosaic* and *pedestrian* mean *ordinary and unimaginative*. *Analogous, commensurate, equivalent,* and *proportional* mean *matching*.
4. **E.** *Deluge* and *inundation* mean *flood*. *Angst, trepidation,* and *disquietude* mean *anxiety;* and *enmity* means *strong dislike*.
5. **B.** "A prosaic (ordinary and unimaginative) essay is probably staid (dull and unadventurous)."
   A. A conventional (ordinary and unimaginative) essay is probably ashen (pale) . . . no.
   B. A pedestrian (ordinary and unimaginative) essay is probably somber (unadventurous) . . . yes.
   C. A negligent (careless) essay is probably taut (tight) . . . no.
   D. An intrepid (brave) essay is probably implicit (complete) . . . no.
   E. An urbane (stylish and charming) essay is probably corresponding (matching) . . . no.
6. **D.** "Serene (calm) is the opposite of disquiet (anxious)."
   A. Commensurate (matching) is the opposite of gossamer (delicate) . . . no.
   B. Equivalent (matching) is the opposite of apathetic (casual, uncaring) . . . no.
   C. Homologous (matching) is the opposite of surreptitious (secret) . . . no.
   D. Consummate (complete) is the opposite of partial . . . yes.
   E. Intrepid (brave) is the opposite of plucky (brave) . . . no.
7. **B.** "If the reservoir overflows, it will equally effect everyone who lives nearby; residents of both the city and the country can expect *overflows* of approximately *equal* size."
   Use the process of elimination, one blank at a time. *Inundations* means *floods,* and *analogous* means *matching*.
8. **B.** "Noka firmly believed that Ben should be admitted into the Honors Program, so he wrote a strong letter of recommendation praising Ben *strongly*."
   Writing the letter may have been a *valiant* (brave) or even *cavalier* (overly casual) thing for Noka to do, but you have evidence only that Noka "firmly believed Ben should get in," and that "he wrote a strong letter." You must base your choice on that evidence, so *unconditionally* (completely) fits best.

Vertigo?

Find each of the following words on the *Breaking Dawn* page number provided. Based on the way each word is used in the book, guess at its definition.

1. **Introspective** (p. 93) might mean _____

_____

2. **Desolation** (p. 105) might mean _____

_____

3. **Rebuff** (p. 107) might mean _____

_____

4. **Torrent** (p. 107) might mean _____

_____

5. **Vertigo** (p. 108) might mean _____

_____

6. **Capital** (p. 110) might mean _____

_____

7. **Premeditation** (p. 110) might mean _____

_____

8. **Equilibrium** (p. 110) might mean _____

_____

Let's see how you did. Check your answers, write the exact definitions,
and reread the sentence in *Breaking Dawn* where each word appears.
Then complete the drills on the next page.

1. **Introspective** (p. 93) means *looking inward* or *thoughtful*. That
   makes sense since *intro-* means *inside,* and you already know
   (from Group 3) that *spect-* means *look,* so *introspective* means
   inside looking—**looking inward, thoughtful.** Synonyms: brooding
   (darkly introspective), contemplative, meditative, musing, pensive,
   reflective, ruminative.

2. **Desolation** (p. 105) means *misery*. It can also mean *emptiness*.
   Determining the meaning of a word from its context is good
   practice. Bella was feeling **miserable,** not **empty,** from the
   vivid dreams. Standardized tests love to use a word with several
   meanings and ask you to determine how it is used in the passage.
   Synonyms: anguish, despair, despondency, wretchedness.

3. **Rebuff** (p. 107) means *refusal.*

4. **Torrent** (p. 107) means *flood* and was a synonym for *deluge* in
   Group 6. The other synonyms are *cascade, cataract, inundation,* and
   spate.

5. **Vertigo** (p. 108) means *dizziness. Vertigo* is sometimes used
   mistakenly to mean *acrophobia* (fear of heights), but it actually
   refers to *dizziness,* such as one might feel when looking down from
   a great height. If you've seen Hitchcock's *Vertigo,* you can picture
   Jimmy Stewart's **dizziness** as he looks down the bell tower.

6. **Capital** (p. 110) in this case means *deserving the death penalty.* It can
   also refer to *uppercase letters, a chief city,* or *money.*

7. **Premeditation** (p. 110) means *planning* and is another interesting
   word to break apart. *Pre-* means *before,* and *meditation* refers to
   thinking or *concentrating,* so *premeditation* means *thinking before*—
   planning.

8. **Equilibrium** (p. 110) means *balance* and can refer to *physical balance*
   (as Bella means it) or *emotional balance. Equi-* means *equal* and *libri-*
   refers to *balance* (that's why the astrological symbol for Libra is the
   scales!), so *equilibrium* means *equal balance*—**balanced!** *Equi-* helps
   you remember high-level vocabulary words such as *equable* (**equal**-
   tempered—calm), *equanimous* (**equal**-tempered—composed), and
   equivocal (**equally** true in several interpretations—unclear).

Synonyms: Select the word or phrase whose meaning is closest to the word in capital letters.

1. INTROSPECTIVE
   - A. ruminative
   - B. anguished
   - C. despairing
   - D. wretched
   - E. despondent

2. DESOLATION
   - A. despondency
   - B. animosity
   - C. antipathy
   - D. disinclination
   - E. enmity

3. TORRENT
   - A. angst
   - B. spate
   - C. trepidation
   - D. disquietude
   - E. impetus

4. PREMEDITATION
   - A. posing
   - B. pleasing
   - C. posting
   - D. pinning
   - E. planning

Analogies: Select the answer choice that best completes the meaning of the sentence.

5. Torrent is to water as
   - A. reverence is to poise
   - B. evanescence is to time
   - C. transience is to laughter
   - D. omniscience is to knowledge
   - E. genteel is to misgivings

6. Rebuff is to agree as
   - A. contemplate is to meditate
   - B. premeditate is to correspond
   - C. commend is to censure
   - D. reproach is to reproof
   - E. foresee is to revere

Sentence Completions: Choose the word that, when inserted in the sentence, best fits the meaning of the sentence as a whole.

7. Vince hoped his explanation was _____, not enigmatic or unclear.
   - A. unequivocal
   - B. capital
   - C. rebuffed
   - D. desolate
   - E. ruminative

8. Selma avoided heights; tall bridges, cliffs, and even scenic overlooks on the highway oftentimes gave her a sense of _____.
   - A. premeditation
   - B. flagellation
   - C. plaudits
   - D. accolades
   - E. vertigo

1. **A.** *Introspective* and *ruminative* mean *looking inward. Anguished, despairing, wretched,* and *despondent* mean *miserable.*
2. **A.** *Desolation* and *despondency* mean *misery. Animosity, antipathy, disinclination,* and *enmity* mean *strong dislike.*
3. **B.** *Torrent* and *spate* mean *flood. Angst, trepidation,* and *disquietude* mean *fear;* and *impetus* means *motivator.*
4. **E.** *Premeditation* means *planning.*
5. **D.** "Torrent is a lot of water."
   A. Reverence (respect) is a lot of poise (composure) . . . no.
   B. Evanescence (temporariness) is a lot of time . . . no.
   C. Transience (temporariness) is a lot of laughter . . . no.
   D. Omniscience (all-knowing) is a lot of knowledge . . . yes.
   E. Genteel (stylish and charming) is a lot of misgivings (doubts) . . . no.
6. **C.** "Rebuff (refuse) is the opposite of agree."
   A. Contemplate (think) is the opposite of meditate (think) . . . no.
   B. Premeditate (plan) is the opposite of correspond (match) . . . no.
   C. Commend (praise) is the opposite of censure (scold) . . . yes.
   D. Reproach (scold) is the opposite of reproof (scold) . . . no.
   E. Foresee (predict) is the opposite of revere (respect) . . . no.
7. **A.** "Vince hoped his explanation was <u>not unclear</u>, not enigmatic or unclear."

   Enigmatic means *mysterious,* but even if you didn't know that word, you could still get this question correct. The SAT often adds a tough word that you don't need into the sentence, so if you see a word in the sentence that you don't know, try crossing it out and doing the question without it. You'll be surprised how well this works! Choice A, *unequivocal,* means *clear and definite* and is the best answer.
8. **E.** "Selma avoided heights; tall bridges, cliffs, and even scenic overlooks on the highway oftentimes gave her a sense of <u>something to be avoided</u>."

   Find evidence and use the process of elimination. The sentence does not indicate that tall bridges, cliffs, and scenic overlooks gave Selma a sense of *premeditation* (planning), *flagellation* (whipping), *plaudits* (praise), or *accolades* (praise). *Vertigo* means *dizziness* and fits best.

Implausible

Find each of the following words on the *Breaking Dawn* page number provided. Based on the way each word is used in the book, guess at its definition.

1. **Dubious** (p. 111) might mean _____

_____

2. **Pretense** (p. 111) might mean _____

_____

3. **Ghosted** (p. 118) might mean _____

_____

4. **Rancid** (p. 121) might mean _____

_____

5. **Avidly** (p. 125) might mean _____

_____

6. **Implausible** (p. 125) might mean _____

_____

7. **Infidelity** (p. 125) might mean _____

_____

8. **Hapless** (p. 126) might mean _____

_____

Let's see how you did. Check your answers, write the exact definitions, and reread the sentence in *Breaking Dawn* where each word appears. Then complete the drills on the next page.

1. **Dubious** (p. 111) in this case means *unreliable*. It can also mean *doubtful* or *hesitant*. Synonyms: fallacious, sophistic, specious, spurious, suspect.

2. **Pretense** (p. 111) means *false display*. Bella describes the word for you, "It wasn't a pretense, Edward. I don't spend *my* free time plotting like some people do"—a *pretense* is a *false plotted display*. Synonyms: facade, guise (like a superhero's disguise), pretext.

3. **Ghosted** (p. 118) means *glided smoothly*, the way Nearly Headless Nick moves in the *Harry Potter* movies.

4. **Rancid** (p. 121) means *spoiled and foul*. Synonyms: fetid, mephitic, miasmic, putrid, rank. These synonyms are high-level vocabulary words, but you can get a sense of their meanings just by asking yourself, "Would I like to be called '_____.'" You may not have known what *fetid* meant, but you probably knew that you didn't want to be called *fetid!* That may give you enough of a sense of the word to get a question correct.

5. **Avidly** (p. 125) means *eagerly*. Synonyms: ardently, fanatically, fervently, keenly, zealously.

6. **Implausible** (p. 125) means *unbelievable*. *Im-* means *not,* and *plausible* means *believable,* so *implausible* means *not believable.*

7. **Infidelity** (p. 125) means *unfaithfulness to a partner.* Just like *im-*, *in-* also means *not,* and since *-fidel* (a little like the French "fidèle" or the Spanish "fiel") refers to *faithful,* you can see why *infidelity* means *unfaithfulness.* *Fidelity* means *trustworthiness,* that's why banks use names like Fidelity National Bank.

8. **Hapless** (p. 126) means *unlucky*.

Synonyms: Select the word or phrase whose meaning is closest to the word in capital letters.

1. DUBIOUS
   A. spurious
   B. rancid
   C. fetid
   D. mephitic
   E. miasmic

2. PRETENSE
   A. infidelity
   B. equilibrium
   C. premeditation
   D. pretext
   E. torrent

3. AVID
   A. fallacious
   B. sophistic
   C. specious
   D. ardent
   E. spurious

4. IMPLAUSIBLE
   A. unbelievable
   B. untrustworthy
   C. hapless
   D. pallid
   E. unconditional

Analogies: Select the answer choice that best completes the meaning of the sentence.

5. Avid is to zealous as
   A. equanimous is to poised
   B. prosaic is to consummate
   C. conventional is to implicit
   D. pedestrian is to sultry
   E. unequivocal is to resolute

6. Hapless is to dubious as
   A. implausible is to modest
   B. rancid is to desolate
   C. tangible is to fervent
   D. unlucky is to spurious
   E. omnipresent is to omniscient

Sentence Completions: Choose the word or words that, when inserted in the sentence, <u>best</u> fits the meaning of the sentence as a whole.

7. On her way to visit Sawyer, Kate _____ past Jack's tent; she walked quietly in hopes of avoiding detection and keeping her traitorous _____ a secret.
   A. rebuffed . . gossamer
   B. flagellated . . vertigo
   C. guffawed . . deluge
   D. catalyzed . . trepidation
   E. ghosted . . infidelity

8. With the _____ of needing to borrow a book, Kyle called Ali, but he was actually hoping that the conversation would lead to a date for the Sigur Rós concert.
   A. pretext
   B. desolation
   C. angst
   D. disquietude
   E. negligence

1. **A.** *Dubious* and *spurious* mean *doubtful. Rancid, fetid, mephitic,* and *miasmic* mean *foul.*
2. **D.** *Pretense* and *pretext* mean *false display. Infidelity* means *unfaithfulness, equilibrium* means *balance, premeditation* means *planning,* and *torrent* means *flood.*
3. **D.** *Avid* and *ardent* mean *eager. Fallacious, sophistic, specious,* and *spurious* mean *unreliable.*
4. **A.** *Implausible* means *unbelievable. Hapless* means *unlucky, pallid* means *pale,* and *unconditional* means *complete.*
5. **A.** "Avid (eager) means the same thing as zealous (eager)."
   - (A.) Equanimous (calm) means the same thing as poised (composed) . . . yes.
   - B . Prosaic (ordinary and unimaginative) means the same thing as consummate (complete) . . . no.
   - C . Conventional (ordinary) means the same thing as implicit (complete) . . . no.
   - D . Pedestrian (ordinary and unimaginative) means the same thing as sultry (hot and humid) . . . no.
   - E . Unequivocal (complete) means the same thing as resolute (brave) . . . no.
6. **D.** Usually the two words in the question are directly related to each other, and the best strategy is to make a sentence that defines one with the other. However, occasionally on the SSAT, the two words are related not to each other but to the two words below. You can recognize this setup when the words in the question are totally unrelated. In that case, set up a relationship to the words in the choices. Choice D is correct since *hapless* means *unlucky,* and *dubious* and *spurious* both mean *unreliable.*
7. **E.** "On her way to visit Sawyer, Kate <u>walked quietly</u> past Jack's tent; she walked quietly in hopes of avoiding detection and keeping her traitorous <u>secret</u> a secret."

   Use the process of elimination, one blank at a time. Cross off words that are **definitely** wrong, and leave choices that could work or that you are unsure of. *Ghosted* means *glided smoothly,* and *infidelity* means *disloyalty.*
8. **A.** "With the <u>excuse</u> of needing to borrow a book, Kyle called Ali, but he was actually hoping that the conversation would lead to a date for the Sigur Rós concert."

   Base your answer on evidence in the sentence. The whole sentence describes a *pretext* (false display): Kyle called "needing to borrow a book," but was "**actually** hoping" that he'd get a date. Not having his book might be a sign of *negligence* (carelessness), but that answer choice does not fit the evidence in the rest of the sentence.

Anguish

Find each of the following words on the *Breaking Dawn* page number provided. Based on the way each word is used in the book, guess at its definition.

1. **Tirade** (p. 135) might mean _____

   _____

2. **Edict** (p. 157) might mean _____

   _____

3. **Hypocrisy** (p. 157) might mean _____

   _____

4. **Loam** (p. 158) might mean _____

   _____

5. **Circumstantial** (p. 160) might mean _____

   _____

6. **Timbre** (p. 162) might mean _____

   _____

7. **Provocation** (p. 162) might mean _____

   _____

8. **Anguish** (p. 171) might mean _____

   _____

Let's see how you did. Check your answers, write the exact definitions, and reread the sentence in *Breaking Dawn* where each word appears. Then complete the drills on the next page.

1. **Tirade** (p. 135) means *angry, attacking speech*. Bella describes it: "Kaure was shouting at him—loudly, furiously, her unintelligible words flying across the room like knives." Yep, that's a **tirade** all right. Synonyms: broadside, diatribe, fulmination, harangue, invective, onslaught, philippic, polemic, rant.

2. **Edict** (p. 157) means *formal declaration*. Jacob cannot disobey an **edict** from the alpha wolf. Synonyms: decree, fiat, mandate, proclamation.

3. **Hypocrisy** (p. 157) means *acting in a different way than one recommends*. Synonym: cant.

4. **Loam** (p. 158) means *rich soil*.

5. **Circumstantial** (p. 160) means *indirect,* and literally comes from the word *circumstance*. It refers to evidence that the **circumstances** imply but do not prove. Good thing the pack is keeping Jacob in check; if he attacked the Cullens now, he might never forgive himself later.

6. **Timbre** (p. 162) means *tone* or *sound quality* and comes from the Greek word for *drum*. Interestingly, *tambour* means *drum* in English and French; in Spanish it's *tambor,* and in Italian it's *tamburo*. Synonym: tenor.

7. **Provocation** (p. 162) in this case means *justification*. It can also mean *deliberate irritation,* as in *being **provoked** to fight*. FYI, standardized tests love the synonyms for that meaning (deliberately irritate to cause action) of *provoke*: foment, goad, incite, prod, spur.

8. **Anguish** (p. 171) means *extreme pain or misery*. Synonyms: agony, desolation, despair, despondency, wretchedness.

Synonyms: Select the word or phrase whose meaning is closest to the word in capital letters.

1. TIRADE
   A. diatribe
   B. edict
   C. decree
   D. fiat
   E. mandate

2. EDICT
   A. hypocrisy
   B. loam
   C. provocation
   D. anguish
   E. mandate

3. PROVOKE
   A. rebuff
   B. reproach
   C. foment
   D. censure
   E. reproof

4. ANGUISH
   A. timbre
   B. hypocrisy
   C. trepidation
   D. desolation
   E. foreboding

Analogies: Select the answer choice that best completes the meaning of the sentence.

5. Loam is to soil as
   A. fulmination is to clay
   B. harangue is to drum
   C. invective is to tambour
   D. philippic is to speech
   E. polemic is to dance

6. Provoke is to goad as
   A. revere is to guffaw
   B. fathom is to ghosting
   C. reproach is to admonish
   D. commend is to increase
   E. presage is to improve

Sentence Completions: Choose the word or words that, when inserted in the sentence, <u>best</u> fits the meaning of the sentence as a whole.

7. Many scholars of the period contend that the Governor's unfair _____ was the largest factor that _____ a revolt among the colonists.
   A. mandate .. anguished
   B. loam .. spurred
   C. polemic .. ghosted
   D. hypocrisy .. soothed
   E. edict .. incited

8. With only flimsy _____ evidence, the prosecutor had little hope of convicting the accused.
   A. circumstantial
   B. hapless
   C. miasmic
   D. capital
   E. reflective

1. **A.** *Tirade* and *diatribe* mean *angry speech*. *Edict, decree, fiat,* and *mandate* mean *formal declaration*.

2. **E.** *Edict* and *mandate* mean *formal declaration*. *Hypocrisy* means *acting in a different way than one recommends,* *loam* means *fertile soil,* *provocation* means *justification,* and *anguish* means *extreme pain*.
3. **C.** *Provoke* and *foment* mean *deliberately irritate*. *Rebuff* means *refuse;* and *reproach, censure,* and *reproof* mean *scold*.
4. **D.** *Anguish* and *desolation* both mean *extreme pain or misery*. *Timbre* means *tone,* *hypocrisy* means *acting in a different way than one recommends,* and *trepidation* and *foreboding* mean *fear*.
5. **D.** "Loam (fertile soil) is a type of soil."
   A. Fulmination (angry speech) is a type of clay . . . no.
   B. Harangue (angry speech) is a type of drum . . . no.
   C. Invective (angry speech) is a type of tambour (drum) . . . no.
   (D.) Philippic (angry speech) is a type of speech . . . yes.
   E. Polemic (angry speech) is a type of dance . . . no.
6. **C.** "Provoke (intentionally irritate) is a synonym for goad (provoke)."
   A. Revere (deeply respect) is a synonym for guffaw (laugh loudly) . . . no.
   B. Fathom (understand) is a synonym for ghosting (gliding smoothly) . . . no.
   (C.) Reproach (scold) is a synonym for admonish (scold) . . . yes.
   D. Commend (praise) is a synonym for increase . . . no.
   E. Presage (predict) is a synonym for improve . . . no.
7. **E.** "Many scholars of the period contend that the Governor's unfair *policy* was the largest factor that *caused* a revolt among the colonists."
   Use the process of elimination, one blank at a time. You can eliminate choice B for the first blank, and you can eliminate choices C and D for the second blank. That leaves only choices A and E. *Edict* means *official declaration,* and *incited* means *provoked,* so choice E is best. The colonists may have been *anguished* (pained), but that word does not fit in the second blank—"anguished a revolt." Make sure your answer choice fits into the blank.
8. **A.** "With only flimsy *flimsy* evidence, the prosecutor had little hope of convicting the accused."
   Circumstantial means *indirect* and is the best choice.

Haggard

Find each of the following words on the *Breaking Dawn* page number provided. Based on the way each word is used in the book, guess at its definition.

1. **Haggard** (p. 171) might mean _____

   _____

2. **Smug** (p. 177) might mean _____

   _____

3. **Conceive** (p. 179) might mean _____

   _____

4. **Incubus** (p. 179) might mean _____

   _____

5. **Succubus** (p. 179) might mean _____

   _____

6. **Prelude** (p. 179) might mean _____

   _____

7. **Venomous** (p. 182) might mean _____

   _____

8. **Rescind** (p. 183) might mean _____

   _____

Let's see how you did. Check your answers, write the exact definitions, and reread the sentence in *Breaking Dawn* where each word appears. Then complete the drills on the next page.

1. **Haggard** (p. 171) means *tired and unhealthy looking*. Even if you have never heard or seen the word *haggard* before, you can determine its meaning from the context—you can tell that Bella looks *tired and unhealthy looking* from the descriptions "deep circles under her eyes," "thinner," and "fragile."

2. **Smug** (p. 177) means *with excessive pride*. Synonyms: arrogant, bombastic, haughty, pompous, supercilious. These are great test-prep words; I saw *bombastic* and *supercilious* on a new SAT just the other day.

3. **Conceive** (p. 179) means *create*. It can mean **create** *a child*, in Edward and Bella's case, or *create an idea,* as in *conceptualize* or *understand*. Synonym: beget.

4. **Incubus** (p. 179) means *male demon that has sex with women in their sleep*. You learned about this when Bella was doing her research in *Twilight* (the first book in the *Twilight* saga) after Jacob told her that the Cullens were vampires. *Incubus* can also mean *a cause of distress*.

5. **Succubus** (p. 179) means *female demon that has sex with men in their sleep*.

6. **Prelude** (p. 179) means *introduction*. You learned in Group 7, from *premeditation*, that *pre-* means *before*. That also helps you understand words such as *precocious* (mature at an early age) and *precipitous* (done **before** careful planning). Synonyms: commencement, overture, precursor.

7. **Venomous** (p. 182) means *very hostile* or *harmful*. Interesting choice of words, Jacob, since *venomous* comes from the word *venom!* The image of Jacob and Bella having a child is a **harmful** "weed" because Jacob knows that if the dream were taken away, he would suffer yet again. Synonyms: baleful, loathsome, maleficent, malevolent, malicious, odious, rancorous.

8. **Rescind** (p. 183) means *take back*. Synonym: revoke.

Synonyms: Select the word or phrase whose meaning is closest to the word in capital letters.

Drills

1. HAGGARD
   - A. evil-looking
   - B. calm-looking
   - C. tired-looking
   - D. nice-looking
   - E. good-looking

2. SMUG
   - A. supercilious
   - B. baleful
   - C. venomous
   - D. maleficent
   - E. rancorous

3. VENOMOUS
   - A. baleful
   - B. bombastic
   - C. haughty
   - D. pompous
   - E. smug

4. RESCIND
   - A. foment
   - B. revoke
   - C. goad
   - D. incite
   - E. prod

Analogies: Select the answer choice that best completes the meaning of the sentence.

5. Venomous is to malicious as
   - A. baleful is to smug
   - B. malevolent is to furtive
   - C. malicious is to haughty
   - D. reverent is to pompous
   - E. supercilious is to bombastic

6. Prelude is to conclusion as
   - A. overture is to edict
   - B. diatribe is to incubus
   - C. provocation is to reaction
   - D. fulmination is to mandate
   - E. invective is to deluge

Sentence Completions: Choose the word that, when inserted in the sentence, <u>best</u> fits the meaning of the sentence as a whole.

7. Rachel is known for her _____ comments, but far from being a succubus, she is actually quite sweet.
   - A. dubious
   - B. venomous
   - C. fallacious
   - D. specious
   - E. spurious

8. The idea for the parade float was _____ by Finn and Mercedes, who developed the concept together.
   - A. rescinded
   - B. fathomed
   - C. commended
   - D. resigned
   - E. conceived

1. **C.** *Haggard* means *tired-looking*. If the correct answer does not jump out, use the process of elimination.

2. **A.** *Smug* and *supercilious* mean with *excessive pride. Baleful, venomous, maleficent,* and *rancorous* mean *very hostile.*

3. **A.** *Venomous* and *baleful* mean *very hostile. Bombastic, haughty, pompous,* and *smug* mean *with excessive pride.*

4. **B.** *Rescind* and *revoke* mean *take back. Foment, goad, incite,* and *prod* mean *provoke.*

5. **E.** "Venomous (very hostile) means the same thing as malicious (very hostile)."
   - A. Baleful (very hostile) means the same thing as smug (with excessive pride) . . . no.
   - B. Malevolent (very hostile) means the same thing as furtive (secret) . . . no.
   - C. Malicious (very hostile) means the same thing as haughty (with excessive pride) . . . no.
   - D. Reverent (deeply respectful) means the same thing as pompous (with excessive pride) . . . no.
   - E. Supercilious (with excessive pride) means the same thing as bombastic (with excessive pride) . . . yes.

6. **C.** "A prelude (introduction) comes before a conclusion."
   - A. An overture (introduction) comes before an edict (formal order) . . . no.
   - B. A diatribe (angry speech) comes before an incubus (male demon) . . . no.
   - C. A provocation (deliberate irritation) comes before a reaction . . . maybe, *provocation* usually gets a reaction.
   - D. A fulmination (angry speech) comes before a mandate (formal order) . . . no.
   - E. An invective (angry speech) comes before a deluge (flood) . . . no.

   Choice C is not perfect, but it is the **best** of the choices.

7. **B.** "Rachel is known for her *not sweet* comments, but far from being a succubus, she is actually quite sweet."

   The sentence tells you that Rachel is **actually** quite sweet, even though she makes not-so-sweet comments. Therefore, *venomous* (very hostile) is the best answer.

8. **E.** "The idea for the parade float was *developed* by Finn and Mercedes, who developed the concept together."

   Use evidence from the sentence—you want a word related to *developed*. Choice E, *conceived,* means *created* and fits best. The idea may have later been *rescinded* (taken back) or *commended* (praised), but you have evidence only that it was "developed."

Solutions

Quiz 2

I. Let's review some of the words that you've seen in Groups 6–10. Match each of the following words to the correct definition or synonym on the right. Then check the solutions on page 171.

1. Prosaic	A. Torrent
2. Deluge	B. Ruminative
3. Corresponding	C. Specious
4. Introspective	D. Pedestrian
5. Desolation	E. Pretext
6. Equilibrium	F. Analogous
7. Dubious	G. Tone
8. Pretense	H. Despair
9. Avid	I. Unhealthy looking
10. Tirade	J. Balance
11. Edict	K. Ardent
12. Timbre	L. Baleful
13. Haggard	M. Supercilious
14. Smug	N. Fiat
15. Venomous	O. Diatribe

II. Let's review several of the word parts that you've seen in Groups 6–10. Match each of the following word parts to the correct definition or synonym on the right. Then check the solutions on page 171.

16. Cor-	A. Before
17. Fidel-	B. Equal
18. Pre-	C. Balance
19. Equi-	D. Not
20. Im-, In-	E. Faithful
21. Libri-	F. Together

Group 11
Abomination?

Find each of the following words on the *Breaking Dawn* page number provided. Based on the way each word is used in the book, guess at its definition.

1. **Hasty** (p. 183) might mean _____

_____

2. **Procreate** (p. 185) might mean _____

_____

3. **Inflection** (p. 186) might mean _____

_____

4. **Sallow** (p. 186) might mean _____

_____

5. **Dementia** (p. 189) might mean _____

_____

6. **Chaos** (p. 199) might mean _____

_____

7. **Circumventing** (p. 199) might mean _____

_____

8. **Abomination** (p. 199) might mean _____

_____

Let's see how you did. Check your answers, write the exact definitions, and reread the sentence in *Breaking Dawn* where each word appears. Then complete the drills on the next page.

Definitions

1. **Hasty** (p. 183) means *rushed.* Synonyms: impetuous, impulsive, rash, temerarious, unpremeditated.

2. **Procreate** (p. 185) sounds like *create* and means *reproduce. Procreate* is a very scientific and polite word for *reproduce;* Jake could have used a slangier word, and in fact, I'm shocked he didn't—quite uncharacteristic of him. I could see a word like that coming from Edward, but not Jacob. Synonyms: breed, propagate.

3. **Inflection** (p. 186) means *change in pitch.* Jacob describes Edward's lack of inflection as "robotic." Synonyms: cadence, intonation, lilt, modulation, timbre.

4. **Sallow** (p. 186) means *pale.* You see a lot of words for *pale* in the *Twilight* saga: *alabaster, ashen, blanched, pallid, sallow,* and *wan.* This is a vampire story after all.

5. **Dementia** (p. 189) refers to *a brain illness involving weakened reasoning, personality changes, and memory loss.* I think Jake is referring specifically to weakened reasoning; given the circumstances, you can see where he's coming from. *De-* means *out,* and *mental* means *of the mind,* so *dementia* literally translates as *out of one's mind.*

6. **Chaos** (p. 199) means *disorder.* Synonyms: anarchy, bedlam, mayhem, pandemonium, turmoil.

7. **Circumventing** (p. 199) means *going around* or *avoiding.* You learned from *circumspect* in Group 3 that *circum-* means *around.* That helps you remember words like *circumscribe* (write **around**— restrict within limits) and *circumlocution* (speaking **around**— speaking vaguely). Synonyms: eluding, prevaricating, equivocating.

8. **Abomination** (p. 199) means *monstrosity,* like the legendary Abominable Snowman. Synonyms: anathema, atrocity, bane, disgrace, horror, outrage.

Synonyms: Select the word or phrase whose meaning is closest to the word in capital letters.

1. HASTY
   A. temerarious
   B. circumspect
   C. maleficent
   D. odious
   E. rancorous

2. INFLECTION
   A. dementia
   B. anarchy
   C. pandemonium
   D. turmoil
   E. cadence

3. SALLOW
   A. circumventing
   B. circumspect
   C. bombastic
   D. wan
   E. haughty

4. ABOMINATION
   A. anathema
   B. prelude
   C. overture
   D. commencement
   E. precursor

Analogies: Select the answer choice that best completes the meaning of the sentence.

5. Abomination is to bane as
   A. atrocity is to timbre
   B. anathema is to mandate
   C. bedlam is to provocation
   D. mayhem is to pandemonium
   E. succubus is to desolation

6. Circumvent is to avoid as
   A. elude is to rescind
   B. prevaricate is to get around
   C. equivocate is to conceive
   D. breed is to foment
   E. propagate is to goad

Sentence Completions: Choose the word or words that, when inserted in the sentence, <u>best</u> fits the meaning of the sentence as a whole.

7. Though Allie suffered from _____, sometimes not remembering her own name, her husband Noah would not allow their children to make _____ and impulsive decisions about her care.
   A. circumlocution .. hasty
   B. inflections .. impetuous
   C. dementia .. rash
   D. anguish .. temerarious
   E. provocation .. unpremeditated

8. Sanja hoped to _____ the rules by talking her way out of the trouble that she was in.
   A. premeditate
   B. circumvent
   C. rescind
   D. circumscribe
   E. circumnavigate

1. **A.** *Hasty* and *temerarious* mean *rushed.* *Circumspect* means *cautious;* and *maleficent, odious,* and *rancorous* mean *hostile.*

2. **E.** *Inflection* and *cadence* mean *pitch.* *Dementia* means *brain illness involving weakened reasoning, personality changes, and memory loss;* and *anarchy, pandemonium,* and *turmoil* mean *disorder.*

3. **D.** *Sallow* and *wan* mean *pale.* If *wan* did not jump right out at you, use the process of elimination. *Circumventing* means *going around, circumspect* means *cautious,* and *bombastic* and *haughty* mean *arrogant.*

4. **A.** *Abomination* and *anathema* mean *monstrosity.* *Prelude, overture, commencement,* and *precursor* mean *introduction.*

5. **D.** "Abomination (monstrosity) means the same thing as bane."
   - A. Atrocity (monstrosity) means the same thing as timbre (tone) . . . no.
   - B. Anathema (monstrosity) means the same thing as mandate (formal command) . . . no.
   - C. Bedlam (chaos) means the same thing as provocation (justification or deliberate irritation) . . . no.
   - (D.) Mayhem (chaos) means the same thing as pandemonium (chaos) . . . yes.
   - E. Succubus (female demon) means the same thing as desolation (misery) . . . no.

6. **B.** "Circumvent means avoid."
   - A. Elude (avoid) means rescind (take back) . . . no.
   - (B.) Prevaricate (avoid) means get around . . . yes.
   - C. Equivocate (avoid) means conceive . . . no.
   - D. Breed (create a child) means foment (provoke) . . . no.
   - E. Propagate (create a child) means goad (provoke) . . . no.

7. **C.** "Though Allie suffered from <u>not remembering her own name</u>, sometimes not remembering her own name, her husband Noah would not allow their children to make <u>impulsive</u> and impulsive decisions about her care."

   Use the process of elimination, one blank at a time. If you can't think of a word to fill a blank, you can look for evidence in the sentence and decide if the word should be positive or negative. Then try the choices, and remember to eliminate only choices that **definitely** do not work. *Dementia* means *mental illness that includes memory loss,* and *rash* means *rushed.*

8. **B.** "Sanja hoped to <u>bend</u> the rules by talking her way out of the trouble that she was in."

   Circumvent means *get around* and fits best. You have not yet learned the word *circumnavigate,* but it means like it sounds like: *circum-* (around) *navigate* (travel), so *travel around,* as in circumnavigate the world.

A Palatable Theory

Find each of the following words on the *Breaking Dawn* page number provided. Based on the way each word is used in the book, guess at its definition.

1. **Synchronization** (p. 199) might mean _____

   _____

2. **Menace** (p. 202) might mean _____

   _____

3. **Bleak** (p. 202) might mean _____

   _____

4. **Forewarned** (p. 222) might mean _____

   _____

5. **Renegade** (p. 225) might mean _____

   _____

6. **Morbid** (p. 241) might mean _____

   _____

7. **Palatable** (p. 242) might mean _____

   _____

8. **Morosely** (p. 264) might mean _____

   _____

Let's see how you did. Check your answers, write the exact definitions, and reread the sentence in *Breaking Dawn* where each word appears. Then complete the drills on the next page.

1. **Synchronization** (p. 199) means *coordination* or *harmony,* like Justin Timberlake, JC Chasez, Joey Fatone, and the other "boys" of 'N Sync. In fact, I think that the wolf-pack boys might make a nice boy band. Since they can hear each other's thoughts they'd be great at those synchronized dance arrangements.

2. **Menace** (p. 202) means *threat,* as in *Star Wars Episode I: The Phantom Menace.* Incidentally, *phantom* means *ghostlike* or *unseen.* Synonyms: hazard, peril.

3. **Bleak** (p. 202) means *grim.*

4. **Forewarned** (p. 222) means *warned in advance. Fore-* means *before* as in *foresight* (see before—*the ability to predict the future*) and *forestall* (stall before—*prevent*).

5. **Renegade** (p. 225) comes from *renege* (break a promise) and means *traitorous.* Traitors have **broken their promises** to be loyal. Synonyms: apostate, dissident, heretical, mutinous, rebellious, treacherous, treasonous.

6. **Morbid** (p. 241) means *gruesome,* as Jake says, "like a horror movie." Synonyms: ghastly, gory, grisly, grotesque, hideous, macabre.

7. **Palatable** (p. 242) means *acceptable* or *pleasant-tasting* and comes from the word *palate* (sense of taste).

8. **Morosely** (p. 264) means *gloomily.* Tough bunch of pages here. You've seen *menace, bleak, morbid,* and *morosely* in a short span of pages. These are tough times for vampires and wolves alike.

Synonyms: Select the word or phrase whose meaning is closest to the word in capital letters.

1. MENACE
   A. catalyst
   B. impetus
   C. precipitant
   D. stimulus
   E. peril

2. RENEGADE
   A. heretical
   B. ghastly
   C. gory
   D. grisly
   E. hideous

3. MORBID
   A. macabre
   B. palatable
   C. synchronized
   D. circumspect
   E. haggard

4. PALATABLE
   A. sallow
   B. ashen
   C. pallid
   D. wan
   E. acceptable

Analogies: Select the answer choice that best completes the meaning of the sentence.

5. Synchronized is to disharmonious as
   A. bleak is to mutinous
   B. menacing is to treacherous
   C. renegade is to loyal
   D. apostate is to palatable
   E. dissident is to morose

6. Forewarned is to surprised as
   A. smug is to baleful
   B. bombastic is to loathsome
   C. supercilious is to malevolent
   D. haughty is to modest
   E. pompous is to odious

Sentence Completions: Choose the word or words that, when inserted in the sentence, best fits the meaning of the sentence as a whole.

7. Throughout the bleak and _____ winter, John Connor battled the _____ of the machines, hoping one day to defeat them and end the threat that they posed to mankind.
   A. grim . . inflection
   B. forewarned . . dementia
   C. morose . . menace
   D. palatable . . chaos
   E. hasty . . turmoil

8. Regina and Gretchen were livid that after they had taught Cady how to be popular, she started a(n) _____ clique that threatened to overtake their group as the most popular one in the school.
   A. impetuous
   B. rash
   C. mutinous
   D. temerarious
   E. unpremeditated

1. **E.** *Menace* and *peril* mean *threat. Catalyst, impetus, precipitant,* and *stimulus* mean *motivator.*

2. **A.** *Renegade* and *heretical* mean *traitorous. Ghastly, gory, grisly,* and *hideous* mean *gruesome.*

3. **A.** *Morbid* and *macabre* mean *gruesome. Palatable* means *acceptable, synchronized* means *harmonized, circumspect* means *cautious,* and *haggard* means *tired-looking.*

4. **E.** *Palatable* means *acceptable. Sallow, ashen, pallid,* and *wan* mean *pale.*

5. **C.** "Synchronized (harmonious) is the opposite of disharmonious (not harmonious)."
   - A. Bleak (grim) is the opposite of mutinous (traitorous) . . . no.
   - B. Menacing (threatening) is the opposite of treacherous . . . no.
   - C. Renegade (traitorous) is the opposite of loyal . . . yes.
   - D. Apostate (traitorous) is the opposite of palatable (acceptable) . . . no.
   - E. Dissident (traitorous) is the opposite of morose (gloomy) . . . no.

6. **D.** "Forewarned (warned in advance) is the opposite of surprised."
   - A. Smug (arrogant) is the opposite of baleful (hostile) . . . no.
   - B. Bombastic (arrogant) is the opposite of loathsome (hostile) . . . no.
   - C. Supercilious (arrogant) is the opposite of malevolent (hostile) . . . no.
   - D. Haughty (arrogant) is the opposite of modest . . . yes.
   - E. Pompous (arrogant) is the opposite of odious (hostile) . . . no.

7. **C.** "Throughout the bleak and *bleak* winter, John Connor battled the *threat* of the machines, hoping one day to defeat them and end the threat that they posed to mankind."

   Use the process of elimination, one blank at a time. Choice C is best, since *morose* means *gloomy,* and *menace* means *threat.*

8. **C.** "Regina and Gretchen were livid that after they had taught Cady how to be popular, she started a(n) *threatening* clique that threatened to overtake their group as the most popular one in the school."

   Mutinous means *traitorous* and fits best. Use evidence in the sentence to choose your answer. Cady may have been rushed (*impetuous, rash, temerarious, unpremeditated*), but you have evidence **only** that she started a new "clique that **threatened** to overtake" Regina and Gretchen's group.

Group 13
Bereft Werewolves

Find each of the following words on the *Breaking Dawn* page number provided. Based on the way each word is used in the book, guess at its definition.

1. **Compensating** (p. 266) might mean _____

   _____

2. **Bereft** (p. 272) might mean _____

   _____

3. **Castoffs** (p. 273) might mean _____

   _____

4. **Somberly** (p. 289) might mean _____

   _____

5. **Belfry** (p. 290) might mean _____

   _____

6. **Placating** (p. 301) might mean _____

   _____

7. **Scornful** (p. 303) might mean _____

   _____

8. **Disdainfully** (p. 303) might mean _____

   _____

Let's see how you did. Check your answers, write the exact definitions, and reread the sentence in *Breaking Dawn* where each word appears. Then complete the drills on the next page.

1. **Compensating** (p. 266) means *making up or paying back for.* Synonyms: rectifying, redressing, indemnifying (compensating for harm or loss).

2. **Bereft** (p. 272) means *without.* The renegade wolves are **without** a home, fresh clothes, and human food. Synonym: sans. *Bereft* can also mean *feeling a strong sense of loss after the death of a loved one.*

3. **Castoffs** (p. 273) means *discards.*

4. **Somberly** (p. 289) means *seriously* or *gloomily.* Synonyms: dolefully, earnestly, gravely, lugubriously, soberly, solemnly.

5. **Belfry** (p. 290) means *bell tower.*

6. **Placating** (p. 301) means *soothing.* Synonyms: abating, allaying, alleviating, ameliorating, appeasing, assuaging, conciliating, mollifying, mitigating, pacifying, palliating, propitiating, tempering. This is definitely one of the SAT's favorite groups of synonyms. Almost every SAT test that I've ever seen (and that is way too many tests) has at least one word from this list. Learn them and you'll gain points!

7. **Scornful** (p. 303) means *harsh and critical.* Question: What are your feelings about Rosalie at this point, loving helper or selfish *termagant* (harsh and bossy woman)? Discuss with your friends. Synonyms: contemptuous, contumelious, derisive, disdainful, disparaging, scathing, sneering, snide.

8. **Disdainfully** (p. 303) means *harshly and critically.* *Disdainful* was a synonym for *scornful,* above. First Rosalie "made a **scornful** noise" and then "sniffed **disdainfully**." She's just not that likable, although she is keeping Bella's baby alive, and Jake is going to owe her a HUGE "thanks" later on. You'll see what I mean . . . . Synonyms: contemptuously, contumeliously, derisively, disdainfully, disparagingly, pejoratively, scathingly, scornfully, sneeringly, snidely.

Synonyms: Select the word or phrase whose meaning is closest to the word in capital letters.

1. COMPENSATING
    A. circumventing
    B. rescinding
    C. indemnifying
    D. prodding
    E. spurring

2. BEREFT
    A. suns
    B. sins
    C. sons
    D. scenes
    E. sans

3. PLACATING
    A. scorning
    B. propitiating
    C. disparaging
    D. scathing
    E. sneering

4. SCORNFUL
    A. doleful
    B. grave
    C. lugubrious
    D. contumelious
    E. solemn

Analogies: Select the answer choice that best completes the meaning of the sentence.

5. Compensating is to rectifying as
    A. redressing is to flagellating
    B. indemnifying is to fathoming
    C. pacifying is to mollifying
    D. allaying is to goading
    E. alleviating is to fomenting

6. Disdainful is to scornful as
    A. contemptuous is to ameliorating
    B. contumelious is to appeasing
    C. derisive is to assuaging
    D. disparaging is to scathing
    E. pejorative is to palliating

Sentence Completions: Choose the word or words that, when inserted in the sentence, best fits the meaning of the sentence as a whole.

7. As the adventurers climbed the stairs up to the _____, they realized the peril they faced, and a grave and _____ mood overtook them.
    A. castoffs .. morose
    B. tower .. zealous
    C. belfry .. somber
    D. menace .. fervent
    E. anathema .. ardent

8. Katniss needed to _____ the audience and regain their support after she had disappointed and angered them.
    A. conciliate
    B. catalyze
    C. harangue
    D. disparage
    E. scorn

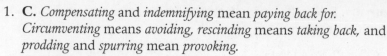

1. **C.** *Compensating* and *indemnifying* mean *paying back for.* *Circumventing* means *avoiding, rescinding* means *taking back,* and *prodding* and *spurring* mean *provoking.*

2. **E.** *Bereft* and *sans* mean *without.*

3. **B.** *Placating* and *propitiating* mean *soothing. Scorning, disparaging, scathing,* and *sneering* mean *criticizing.*

4. **D.** *Scornful* and *contumelious* mean *harsh and critical.* Cross off answers that you are **sure** don't work, and then choose the best of what is left. Choices A, B, C, and E mean *serious or gloomy.*

5. **C.** "Compensating (paying back for) means rectifying (making up for)."
   A. Redressing (paying back for) means flagellating (whipping) . . . no.
   B. Indemnifying (paying back for) means fathoming (understanding) . . . no.
   C. Pacifying (soothing) means mollifying (soothing) . . . yes.
   D. Allaying (soothing) means goading (provoking) . . . no.
   E. Alleviating (soothing) means fomenting (provoking) . . . no.

6. **D.** "Disdainful (harsh and critical) is a synonym of scornful."
   A. Contemptuous (harsh and critical) is a synonym of ameliorating (soothing) . . . no.
   B. Contumelious (harsh and critical) is a synonym of appeasing (soothing) . . . no.
   C. Derisive (harsh and critical) is a synonym of assuaging (soothing) . . . no.
   D. Disparaging (harsh and critical) is a synonym of scathing (harsh and critical) . . . yes.
   E. Pejorative (harsh and critical) is a synonym of palliating (soothing) . . . no.

7. **C.** "As the adventurers climbed the stairs up to the <u>top of the stairs</u>, they realized the peril they faced, and a grave and <u>grave</u> mood overtook them."
   Choice C works best. *Belfry* means *bell tower,* and *somber* means *serious.* Choice B, *zealous* (eager), does not fit the evidence. The sentence gives evidence that the adventurers were *grave* (serious), not *eager.*

8. **A.** "Katniss needed to <u>regain</u> the audience and regain their support after she had disappointed and angered them."
   Conciliate means *soothe* and works best. *Catalyze* means *motivate,* which could be a way to "regain their support," but *conciliate* (soothe) more directly fits the evidence that "she had disappointed and angered them."

Group 14

Flabbergasted

Find each of the following words on the *Breaking Dawn* page number provided. Based on the way each word is used in the book, guess at its definition.

1. **Indifferent** (p. 303) might mean _____

   _____

2. **Reconnaissance** (p. 309) might mean _____

   _____

3. **Yoga** (p. 313) might mean _____

   _____

4. **Loping** (p. 313) might mean _____

   _____

5. **Pedigree** (p. 319) might mean _____

   _____

6. **Figurative** (p. 319) might mean _____

   _____

7. **Vicariously** (p. 320) might mean _____

   _____

8. **Flabbergasted** (p. 325) might mean _____

   _____

Let's see how you did. Check your answers, write the exact definitions, and reread the sentence in *Breaking Dawn* where each word appears. Then complete the drills on the next page.

1. **Indifferent** (p. 303) means *unconcerned* or *uncaring*. *In-* means *not*, so *indifferent* means *not showing a difference—not caring*. *Indifferent* was a synonym for *blasé* in Group 3. Synonyms: apathetic, cavalier, dismissive, dispassionate, impassive, insouciant, nonchalant, perfunctory. The SAT also loves testing the antonym *solicitous* (concerned), which is the opposite of *indifferent*.

2. **Reconnaissance** (p. 309) comes from the word *recognizing* and means *scouting* or *exploring*. Jake, Seth, and Leah are on a **scouting** mission (checking if they **recognize** any wolf scents) to see if it's safe for the Cullens to go hunting.

3. **Yoga** (p. 313) refers to *Indian physical and spiritual exercises aimed at achieving enlightenment*. Yoga is also used for stress management, and Leah **definitely** needs some of that!

4. **Loping** (p. 313) means *running or jogging with a graceful stride*. This word has a very specific meaning in horseback riding, where *lope* is a slower variation of *canter* used in Western riding.

5. **Pedigree** (p. 319) means *ancestry*. Synonyms: bloodline, descent, genealogy, heritage, lineage.

6. **Figurative** (p. 319) means *not literal*. Leah means that while Rosalie is **literally** cold (because she's a vampire), she is also **figuratively** cold (uncaring, indifferent) because she's "focused" on helping Bella have the baby.

7. **Vicariously** (p. 320) means *through someone else*. Leah means that Rosalie wants a baby but can't have one, so by helping Bella she is experiencing what it's like to have a baby **through someone else's eyes.**

8. **Flabbergasted** (p. 325) means *astonished*. *Flabbergasted* does not have Latin word parts and can't even be broken down. *Flabber* and *gasted* are gibberish, yet the word gives you a hint, and even sounds like what it means. Picture someone flabbergasted, standing with mouth *agape* (wide open), staring straight ahead, **astonished.** Synonyms: boggled, confounded, dumbfounded, staggered, stupefied.

Synonyms: Select the word or phrase whose meaning is closest to the word in capital letters.

1. INDIFFERENT
   A. insouciant
   B. figurative
   C. confounded
   D. stupefied
   E. boggled

2. PEDIGREE
   A. yoga
   B. lineage
   C. castoffs
   D. reconnaissance
   E. contempt

3. VICARIOUS
   A. with someone else
   B. near someone else
   C. alone
   D. through someone else
   E. without someone else

4. FLABBERGASTED
   A. confounded
   B. figurative
   C. loping
   D. apathetic
   E. cavalier

Analogies: Select the answer choice that best completes the meaning of the sentence.

5. Indifferent is to solicitous as
   A. loping is to running
   B. heretical is to morbid
   C. renegade is to palatable
   D. apostate is to macabre
   E. figurative is to literal

6. Heritage is to lineage as
   A. compensating is to contemptuous
   B. impassive is to scornful
   C. insouciant is to contumelious
   D. nonchalant is to disparaging
   E. perfunctory is to apathetic

Sentence Completions: Choose the word that, when inserted in the sentence, best fits the meaning of the sentence as a whole.

7. Gregory appreciated his mother's _____ calls checking up on his well-being.
   A. indifferent
   B. perfunctory
   C. insouciant
   D. solicitous
   E. pejorative

8. Jacob is alpha wolf because of his _____; his bloodline can be traced straight to the first werewolf of the tribe.
   A. descent
   B. reconnaissance
   C. indifference
   D. catalyst
   E. inflection

1. **A.** *Indifferent* and *insouciant* mean *unconcerned*. *Figurative* means *not literal;* and *confounded, stupefied,* and *boggled* mean *astonished*.

2. **B.** *Pedigree* and *lineage* mean *ancestry*. *Yoga* means *Indian spiritual exercises, castoffs* means *discards, reconnaissance* means *scouting,* and *contempt* means *harsh criticism*.

3. **D.** *Vicarious* means *through someone else*.

4. **A.** *Flabbergasted* and *confounded* mean *astonished. Figurative* means *not literal, loping* means *running gracefully,* and *apathetic* and *cavalier* mean *unconcerned*.

5. **E.** "Indifferent (unconcerned) is the opposite of solicitous (concerned)."
   A. Loping (running) is the opposite of running . . . no.
   B. Heretical (traitorous) is the opposite of morbid (gloomy) . . . no.
   C. Renegade (traitorous) is the opposite of palatable (acceptable) . . . no.
   D. Apostate (traitorous) is the opposite of macabre (gruesome) . . . no.
   E. Figurative (not literal) is the opposite of literal . . . yes.

6. **E.** "Heritage (ancestors) means the same thing as lineage."
   A. Compensating (paying back for) means the same thing as contemptuous (harsh and critical) . . . no.
   B. Impassive (uncaring) means the same thing as scornful (harsh and critical) . . . no.
   C. Insouciant (uncaring) means the same thing as contumelious (harsh and critical) . . . no.
   D. Nonchalant (uncaring) means the same thing as disparaging (harsh and critical) . . . no.
   E. Perfunctory (uncaring) means the same thing as apathetic (uncaring) . . . yes.

7. **D.** "Gregory appreciated his mother's _checking up_ calls checking up on his well-being."

   The evidence in the sentence tells you that Gregory's mom was "checking up on his well-being," so *solicitous* (concerned) is the best choice.

8. **A.** "Jacob is alpha wolf because of his _bloodline;_ his bloodline can be traced straight to the first werewolf of the tribe."

   Descent and *bloodline* mean *ancestry*. Remember to think of a word you want to fill the blank before you look at the choices, and choose a word right from the sentence when possible.

Group 15
Fanatical Adoration

Find each of the following words on the *Breaking Dawn* page number provided. Based on the way each word is used in the book, guess at its definition.

1. **Incredulous** (p. 326) might mean _____

_____

2. **Fanatical** (p. 326) might mean _____

_____

3. **Adoration** (p. 326) might mean _____

_____

4. **Crooned** (p. 326) might mean _____

_____

5. **Loathsome** (p. 327) might mean _____

_____

6. **Melodramatic** (p. 335) might mean _____

_____

7. **Averse** (p. 337) might mean _____

_____

8. **Facilities** (p. 339) might mean _____

_____

Let's see how you did. Check your answers, write the exact definitions, and reread the sentence in *Breaking Dawn* where each word appears. Then complete the drills on the next page.

Definitions

1. **Incredulous** (p. 326) means *unbelieving*. *Cred-* refers to *believe*, and of course *in-*, like *un-*, means *not*, so you can see why *incredulous* means *unbelieving* or *doubting*. Synonym: dubious.

2. **Fanatical** (p. 326) means *extremely devoted*. Synonyms: ardent, avid, compulsive, fervent, fervid, keen, zealous.

3. **Adoration** (p. 326) comes from *adore* and means *love* or *worship*. Synonyms: reverence, veneration.

4. **Crooned** (p. 326) means *hummed or sung softly* and was a synonym for *warble* and *trill* in Group 2. The related word *crooner* is *a singer who sings sentimental songs in a low, sweet voice.* Famous crooners include Frank Sinatra, Nat King Cole, and (still keeping crooning alive) Morrissey.

5. **Loathsome** (p. 327) means *repulsive* or *worthy of hatred*. Notice that Stephenie Meyer italicized "adores" in a previous line. The SAT and ACT love to ask why a word in a passage is italicized. In this case, it is to show that the word is emphasized when read. Sometimes, however, it is used to indicate that the word is used ironically. In that case, "He absolutely *adores* you" would mean *he loathes (hates) you*. *Adore* and *loathe* are opposites. You can tell which meaning an author intends from the words and sentences around the italicized word.

6. **Melodramatic** (p. 335) means *very dramatic*. You probably knew or could have guessed that, but I included this word to bring up the synonyms *histrionic* and *operatic*. Standardized tests love to use these words. Most students don't know them, but now you do, thanks to Jake's **dramatic** quest to imprint. Interestingly, *histrion* is one of the words for *clown* in French, and clowns are pretty **dramatic.**

7. **Averse** (p. 337) means *opposed to*.

8. **Facilities** (p. 339) in this case means *abilities*. Synonyms: aptitudes, capacities, faculties, prowess.

Synonyms: Select the word or phrase whose meaning is closest to the word in capital letters.

1. FANATICAL
   A. loathsome
   B. melodramatic
   C. zealous
   D. operatic
   E. histrionic

2. ADORATION
   A. pedigree
   B. descent
   C. genealogy
   D. lineage
   E. veneration

3. LOATHSOME
   A. avid
   B. compulsive
   C. repulsive
   D. fervent
   E. keen

4. MELODRAMATIC
   A. histrionic
   B. averse
   C. dubious
   D. incredulous
   E. ardent

Analogies: Select the answer choice that best completes the meaning of the sentence.

5. Histrionic is to equanimous as
   A. loathsome is to odious
   B. melodramatic is to operatic
   C. fanatical is to insouciant
   D. haggard is to futile
   E. surreptitious is to clandestine

6. Facilities is to aptitudes as
   A. guffaws is to nuptials
   B. spectacles is to qualms
   C. hordes is to kudos
   D. legions is to dispositions
   E. accolades is to plaudits

Sentence Completions: Choose the word that, when inserted in the sentence, best fits the meaning of the sentence as a whole.

7. Alex had a(n) _____ adoration for each of his many pursuits; whatever he did, he did with ardent enthusiasm.
   A. zealous
   B. averse
   C. polarized
   D. serene
   E. tranquil

8. The audience was _____ that Natalia, a six-year-old, had painted such an advanced work of art and demanded to meet the alleged artist.
   A. crooning
   B. fanatical
   C. loathsome
   D. goading
   E. incredulous

1. **C.** *Fanatical* and *zealous* mean *extremely devoted*. *Loathsome* means *repulsive;* and *melodramatic, operatic,* and *histrionic* mean *very dramatic*.

2. **E.** *Adoration* and *veneration* mean *love* or *worship*. *Pedigree, descent, genealogy,* and *lineage* mean *ancestry*.

3. **C.** *Loathsome* means *repulsive*. *Avid, compulsive, fervent,* and *keen* mean *extremely devoted*.

4. **A.** *Melodramatic* and *histrionic* mean *very dramatic*. If you're not sure, use the process of elimination—cross off answers that you are **sure** don't work and choose the best of what's left. *Averse* means *opposed to, dubious* and *incredulous* mean *doubtful,* and *ardent* means *eager* or *extremely devoted*.

5. **C.** "Histrionic (very dramatic) is the opposite of equanimous (calm)."
   - A. Loathsome (repulsive) is the opposite of odious (hostile) . . . no.
   - B. Melodramatic (very dramatic) is the opposite of operatic (very dramatic) . . . no.
   - (C.) Fanatical (extremely devoted) is the opposite of insouciant (uncaring) . . . yes.
   - D. Haggard (unhealthy looking) is the opposite of futile (useless) . . . no.
   - E. Surreptitious (secret) is the opposite of clandestine (secret) . . . no.

6. **E.** "Facilities (abilities) means the same thing as aptitudes."
   - A. Guffaws (loud laughs) means the same thing as nuptials (wedding) . . . no.
   - B. Spectacles (something interesting to look at) means the same thing as qualms (doubts) . . . no.
   - C. Hordes (mobs) means the same thing as kudos (praise) . . . no.
   - D. Legions (associations of lots of people) means the same thing as dispositions (ways of being) . . . no.
   - (E.) Accolades (praise) means the same thing as plaudits (praise) . . . yes.

7. **A.** "Alex had a(n) <u>*ardent*</u> adoration for each of his many pursuits; whatever he did, he did with ardent enthusiasm."
   Zealous and *ardent* mean *extremely devoted* or *eager*.

8. **E.** "The audience was <u>*surprised*</u> that Natalia, a six-year-old, had painted such an advanced work of art and demanded to meet the alleged artist."
   Incredulous means *doubtful*. The audience was *doubtful,* which is why they "demanded to meet the *alleged* (supposed) artist."

Quiz 3

I. Let's review some of the words that you've seen in Groups 11–15. Match each of the following words to the correct definition or synonym on the right. Then check the solutions on page 171.

1. Hasty		A.	Wan
2. Sallow		B.	Dissident
3. Circumventing		C.	Ameliorate
4. Menace		D.	Temerarious
5. Renegade		E.	Pejorative
6. Morbid		F.	Peril
7. Compensate		G.	Going around
8. Placate		H.	Scouting
9. Disdainful		I.	Veneration
10. Indifferent		J.	Macabre
11. Reconnaissance		K.	Insouciant
12. Pedigree		L.	Indemnify
13. Fanatical		M.	Histrionic
14. Adoration		N.	Zealous
15. Melodramatic		O.	Lineage

II. Let's review several of the word parts that you've seen in Groups 11–15. Match each of the following word parts to the correct definition or synonym on the right. Then check the solutions on page 171.

16. Circum-		A.	Before
17. Fore-		B.	Believe
18. In-, Un-		C.	Around
19. Cred-		D.	Out
20. De-		E.	Of the mind
21. Mental		F.	Not

Proactive

Find each of the following words on the *Breaking Dawn* page number provided. Based on the way each word is used in the book, guess at its definition.

1. **Eventuality** (p. 340) might mean _____

   _____

2. **Proactive** (p. 341) might mean _____

   _____

3. **Comrade** (p. 341) might mean_____

   _____

4. **Condemn** (p. 342) might mean _____

   _____

5. **Absolve** (p. 342) might mean _____

   _____

6. **Fervent** (p. 345) might mean _____

   _____

7. **Ferocity** (p. 351) might mean _____

   _____

8. **Hyperaware** (p. 353) might mean _____

   _____

Let's see how you did. Check your answers, write the exact definitions, 65
and reread the sentence in *Breaking Dawn* where each word appears.
Then complete the drills on the next page.

Definitions

1. **Eventuality** (p. 340) means *possibility*. This is a terrific high-level
   vocabulary word that people rarely use, but leave it to Edward to
   toss out high-level SAT vocab! Spend some time around Edward
   and your SAT scores are sure to rise. Synonym: contingency.

2. **Proactive** (p. 341) means *acting in advance of something, rather than
   as a reaction after it has happened*. In this case, *pro-* means *before*, so
   before active—*in advance*. *Pro-* can also mean *much*, as in *prodigious*
   (enormous), *prolix* (too wordy), and *prolific* (plentiful). Stephenie
   Meyer has produced a **prodigious** amount of writing. In only five
   years, she has published almost 2,500 pages of the *Twilight* saga—
   truly **prolific.**

3. **Comrade** (p. 341) means *companion*, and *"comrade in arms"* means
   fellow soldier.

4. **Condemn** (p. 342) means *officially denounce*. Synonyms: castigate,
   censure, excoriate, rebuke, reproach (less strong disapproval), reprove.
   Very *malicious* (mean) condemnation is called *vituperative*. That word
   even sounds mean—my face tightens as I say it.

5. **Absolve** (p. 342) means *declare free of blame* and is the opposite of
   condemn—I see an analogy question coming. As Ephraim's heir,
   Jacob has the power to **officially denounce** or **free** the Cullens
   of blame. Synonyms: acquit, exculpate, exonerate, pardon,
   vindicate. You hear some of these words in crime dramas such
   as *CSI* and *NCIS*.

6. **Fervent** (p. 345) means *passionate*. You saw this word as a synonym
   for *avid* in Group 8 and *fanatical* in Group 15. Synonyms: ardent,
   compulsive, fervid, keen, zealous.

7. **Ferocity** (p. 351) comes from the word *ferocious,* which comes from
   the word *fierce* and can mean *hostility, bitterness,* or *determination.* I
   think Edward was feeling mostly *determined* in this instance.

8. **Hyperaware** (p. 353) means *very aware*. You guessed it, *hyper-*
   means *very*, as in *hyperactive* (very active or overactive) or *hyperbole*
   (very exaggerated statement).

Synonyms: Select the word or phrase whose meaning is closest to the word in capital letters.

1. EVENTUALITY
   A. comrade
   B. ferocity
   C. contingency
   D. hyperbole
   E. veneration

2. CONDEMN
   A. acquit
   B. exonerate
   C. exculpate
   D. pardon
   E. censure

3. ABSOLVE
   A. vindicate
   B. croon
   C. placate
   D. allay
   E. ameliorate

4. FERVENT
   A. omniscient
   B. pejorative
   C. proactive
   D. keen
   E. contumelious

Analogies: Select the answer choice that best completes the meaning of the sentence.

5. Absolve is to condemn as
   A. mollify is to assuage
   B. alleviate is to palliate
   C. pacify is to aggravate
   D. placate is to appease
   E. allay is to abate

6. Hyperaware is to blasé as
   A. surreptitious is to furtive
   B. sly is to clandestine
   C. debonair is to genteel
   D. urbane is to crude
   E. futile is to vain

Sentence Completions: Choose the word that, when inserted in the sentence, <u>best</u> fits the meaning of the sentence as a whole.

7. After a supervisor commented on Mike's insouciant attitude at work, Mike took on a much more _____ enthusiasm toward his work tasks.
   A. ardent
   B. apathetic
   C. dismissive
   D. insouciant
   E. perfunctory

8. Juanita hoped that her new formal gown with gossamer straps would _____ her and win public approval after the press ridiculed her outfit at last year's award ceremony.
   A. condemn
   B. censure
   C. vindicate
   D. rebuke
   E. reprove

1. **C.** *Eventuality* and *contingency* mean *possibility. Comrade* means companion; *and ferocity* means *hostility, bitterness,* or *determination. Hyperbole* means *very exaggerated statement,* and *veneration* means *deep respect.*

2. **E.** *Condemn* and *censure* mean *officially denounce. Acquit, exonerate, exculpate,* and *pardon* mean *free from blame.*

3. **A.** *Absolve* and *vindicate* mean *free from blame. Croon* means *sing sweetly;* and *placate, allay,* and *ameliorate* mean *soothe.*

4. **D.** *Fervent* and *keen* mean *passionate. Omniscient* means *all-knowing, pejorative* means *harsh and critical, proactive* means *acting in advance,* and *contumelious* means *harsh and critical.*

5. **C.** "Absolve (free from blame) is the opposite of condemn (formally denounce)."
   A. Mollify (soothe) is the opposite of assuage (soothe) . . . no.
   B. Alleviate (soothe) is the opposite of palliate (soothe) . . . no.
   (C.) Pacify (soothe) is the opposite of aggravate . . . yes.
   D. Placate (soothe) is the opposite of appease (soothe) . . . no.
   E. Allay (soothe) is the opposite of abate (soothe) . . . no.

6. **D.** "Hyperaware (very aware) is the opposite of blasé (bored and uncaring)."
   A. Surreptitious (secret) is the opposite of furtive (secret) . . . no.
   B. Sly (secret) is the opposite of clandestine (secret) . . . no.
   C. Debonair (stylish and charming) is the opposite of genteel (stylish and charming) . . . no.
   (D.) Urbane (stylish and charming) is the opposite of crude . . . yes.
   E. Futile (useless) is the opposite of vain (useless) . . . no.

7. **A.** "After a supervisor commented on Mike's insouciant attitude at work, Mike took on a much more _non-insouciant_ enthusiasm toward his work tasks."
   Ardent means *eager* and fits best. Use the process of elimination one blank at a time. Cross off words that are **definitely** wrong, leave words that are even somewhat possible, and choose the best of the remaining choices. Also, if there is a word, such as *insouciant* (uncaring), that you don't know in the question, cross it out and try without it. Usually you don't need any one specific word to get a question correct!

8. **C.** "Juanita hoped that her new formal gown with gossamer straps would _win public approval for_ her and win public approval after the press ridiculed her outfit at last years award ceremony."
   Vindicate means *free from blame* and is the best answer.

Group 17
Congealing Blood

Find each of the following words on the *Breaking Dawn* page number provided. Based on the way each word is used in the book, guess at its definition.

1. **Congealing** (p. 354) might mean _____

   _____

2. **Viscous** (p. 354) might mean _____

   _____

3. **Inferno** (p. 357) might mean _____

   _____

4. **Aberration** (p. 357) might mean _____

   _____

5. **Reanimate** (p. 358) might mean _____

   _____

6. **Complement** (p. 372) might mean _____

   _____

7. **Atlas** (p. 374) might mean _____

   _____

8. **Obliterated** (p. 374) might mean _____

   _____

Let's see how you did. Check your answers, write the exact definitions, and reread the sentence in *Breaking Dawn* where each word appears. Then complete the drills on the next page.

1. **Congealing** (p. 354) means *coming together.* Remember that *con-* means *together,* so this word means *gelling together*—definitely a word that means what it sounds like. Synonyms: amalgamating, coalescing, converging, fusing, homogenizing.

2. **Viscous** (p. 354) means *thick and gooey.* Jacob describes this word in the previous sentence: the blood "was congealing," and it was "thicker and slower" moving—that's **viscous** (thick and gooey). Students often confuse this word with *vicious* (cruel, like Jane and Alec). Synonyms: gelatinous, glutinous, mucilaginous, treacly.

3. **Inferno** (p. 357) means *massive fire.*

4. **Aberration** (p. 357) means *abnormality;* Jacob describes this when he says, "its existence went against nature." Synonyms: anomaly, deviation, divergence, perversion.

5. **Reanimate** (p. 358) means *revive* or *bring back to life.* *Re-* means *again,* and *animate* means *with life or spirit,* so *reanimate* means *again with life—bring back to life.* These word parts can help you remember the high-level SAT word *pusill**animous**,* which means *very shy* and comes from *pusill* (small) and *animus* (spirit)— *unspirited,* **very shy.**

6. **Complement** (p. 372) means *amount.* Synonym: contingent (remember from Group 16 that *contingency* can also mean *possibility*). The word *compliment,* spelled with an *i,* means *praise.*

7. **Atlas** (p. 374) refers to the *mythological Greek god who holds up the heavens (planets).* Bella says she's not Atlas and can't shoulder the blackness, which "felt as heavy as a planet."

8. **Obliterated** (p. 374) means *totally destroyed.* This page in *Breaking Dawn* gives a clue to Bella's future vampire gift. I won't tell you the gift, but here's the clue on the page: "It was sort of the pattern to my life . . . . The only thing I'd ever been able to do was keep going. Endure. Survive." Synonyms: annihilated, decimated, eradicated, expunged.

Synonyms: Select the word or phrase whose meaning is closest to the word in capital letters.

1. CONGEAL
   A. amalgamate
   B. reanimate
   C. compliment
   D. obliterate
   E. decimate

2. VISCOUS
   A. pusillanimous
   B. annihilated
   C. eradicated
   D. expunged
   E. mucilaginous

3. INFERNO
   A. massive flood
   B. huge fire
   C. powerful wind
   D. large earthquake
   E. small pebbles

4. ABBERATION
   A. Atlas
   B. complement
   C. coalescing
   D. anomaly
   E. homogenizing

Analogies: Select the answer choice that best completes the meaning of the sentence.

5. Aberration is to divergence as
   A. histrionics is to inflection
   B. adoration is to reconnaissance
   C. reverence is to disdain
   D. veneration is to menace
   E. eventuality is to contingency

6. Obliterated is to conceived as
   A. eradicated is to created
   B. reanimated is to censured
   C. congealed is to condemned
   D. fused is to rebuked
   E. amalgamated is to reproved

Sentence Completions: Choose the words that, when inserted in the sentence, <u>best</u> fits the meaning of the sentence as a whole.

7. The viscous fluid created in the science experiment was _____ of several components, from motor oil to maple syrup.
   A. an obliteration
   B. a perversion
   C. an anomaly
   D. an amalgamation
   E. a reanimation

8. Jordan believed that the best choreography involved _____ of styles, a convergence of everything from ballet to hip-hop.
   A. an inferno
   B. a divergence
   C. a fusion
   D. a cadence
   E. an eventuality

1. **A.** *Congeal* and *amalgamate* both mean *come together. Reanimate* means *revive; compliment* means *praise;* and *obliterate* and *decimate* mean *totally destroy.*

2. **E.** *Viscous* and *mucilaginous* mean *thick and gooey. Pusillanimous* means *very shy;* and *annihilated, eradicated,* and *expunged* mean *totally destroyed.*

3. **B.** *Inferno* means *huge fire.*

4. **D.** *Aberration* and *anomaly* mean *abnormality. Atlas* refers to *a Greek god, complement* means *amount,* and *coalescing* and *homogenizing* mean *coming together. Homo-* means *same,* so *homogenizing* means *making all of something the same* (coming together).

5. **E.** "Aberration (abnormality) means divergence."
   - A. Histrionics (dramatics) means inflection (change in pitch) . . . no.
   - B. Adoration (deep respect) means reconnaissance (scouting) . . . no.
   - C. Reverence (deep respect) means disdain (hatred) . . . no.
   - D. Veneration (deep respect) means menace (threat) . . . no.
   - (E.) Eventuality (possibility) means contingency (possibility) . . . yes.

   Histrionics (dramatics) may or may not involve a *change in pitch,* but *eventuality* definitely means *contingency.*

6. **A.** "Obliterated (totally destroyed) is the opposite of conceived (created)."
   - (A.) Eradicated (totally destroyed) is the opposite of created . . . yes.
   - B. Reanimated (revived) is the opposite of censured (officially denounced) . . . no.
   - C. Congealed (came together) is the opposite of condemned (officially denounced) . . . no.
   - D. Fused (came together) is the opposite of rebuked (officially denounced) . . . no.
   - E. Amalgamated (came together) is the opposite of reproved (officially denounced) . . . no.

7. **D.** "The viscous fluid created in the science experiment was a *creation* of several components, from motor oil to maple syrup."
   Amalgamation means *coming together* or *mixture* and fits best.

8. **C.** "Jordan believed that the best choreography involved a *convergence* of styles, a convergence of everything from ballet to hip-hop."
   Fusion and *convergence* mean *bringing together. Cadence* (change in pitch) has to do with the musical theme of the sentence, but does not fit the blank. That's why you think of a word you'd like to see before you look at the choices.

Excruciating Combustion

Find each of the following words on the *Breaking Dawn* page number provided. Based on the way each word is used in the book, guess at its definition.

1. **Phantom** (p. 375) might mean _____

_____

2. **Resolve** (p. 380) might mean _____

_____

3. **Berating** (p. 380) might mean _____

_____

4. **Flog** (p. 381) might mean _____

_____

5. **Sanguine** (p. 382) might mean _____

_____

6. **Razed** (p. 383) might mean _____

_____

7. **Excruciating** (p. 384) might mean _____

_____

8. **Combustible** (p. 385) might mean _____

_____

Let's see how you did. Check your answers, write the exact definitions, and reread the sentence in *Breaking Dawn* where each word appears. Then complete the drills on the next page.

1. **Phantom** (p. 375) means *ghostlike* or *unseen*. I mentioned this word in Group 12 with *Star Wars Episode I: The Phantom Menace*. This is also a word you hear quite a bit on *Ghost Hunters,* such as when Steve Gonsalves tells Dave Tango, "Well, you've come a long way, that's for sure . . . . I remember you were running around that basement in Jersey thinking everything was a ghost; every smell was a **phantom** smell." (SyFy, "Stanley Hotel," 2004)

2. **Resolve** (p. 380) means *determination*. Synonyms: grit, moxie, perseverance, pertinacity, pluck, tenacity.

3. **Berating** (p. 380) means *scolding angrily*. Synonyms: admonishing, censuring, chiding, rebuking, reprimanding, reproaching, reproofing.

4. **Flog** (p. 381) means *whip*. *Flog* actually comes from the word *flagellate* (whip), which you learned in Group 5. I doubt Edward actually wants to *whip* anyone (well, okay, maybe he does want to whip Jacob), but "flog" is the kind of discipline language that Edward might have heard used when he was a kid back in the early 1900s. He probably just means that he wants to give Rosalie and Jacob a *stern* (serious) talking-to.

5. **Sanguine** (p. 382) means *optimistic and cheerful*. Interestingly, it can also refer to a ***blood**-red color!* That's because *sanguin-* means *blood*. The connection is that **optimistic and cheerful** people usually have **red,** rosy cheeks, and red and rosy cheeks are that color because they are flushed with **blood!** Synonyms: buoyant, ebullient.

6. **Razed** (p. 383) means *destroyed*. *Razed* reminds me of *obliterated* from Group 17. Synonyms: annihilated, demolished.

7. **Excruciating** (p. 384) means *unbearable,* as in the *Cruciatus Curse* that Voldemort uses in the *Harry Potter* books and movies to inflict **unbearable** pain. Synonym: agonizing.

8. **Combustible** (p. 385) means *burnable*. Synonyms: flammable, ignitable, incendiary.

74 **Synonyms:** Select the word or phrase whose meaning is closest to the word in capital letters.

Drills

1. RESOLVE
   A. phantom
   B. combustion
   C. tenacity
   D. fusion
   E. amalgamation

2. BERATE
   A. combust
   B. ignite
   C. annihilate
   D. demolish
   E. censure

3. SANGUINE
   A. ebullient
   B. morose
   C. doleful
   D. lugubrious
   E. solemn

4. RAZE
   A. flog
   B. admonish
   C. censure
   D. chide
   E. demolish

Analogies: Select the answer choice that best completes the meaning of the sentence.

5. Surreptitious is to phantom as
   A. clandestine is to ebullient
   B. furtive is to covert
   C. resolute is to excruciating
   D. sanguine is to incendiary
   E. buoyant is to pejorative

6. Pusillanimous is to resolve as
   A. incendiary is to grit
   B. very shy is to moxie
   C. very smart is to pertinacity
   D. sanguine is to pluck
   E. ebullient is to viscosity

Sentence Completions: Choose the word or words that, when inserted in the sentence, <u>best</u> fits the meaning of the sentence as a whole.

7. In order to forestall the town's planned _____ of the historic district, Akiko raised over $10,000 to help _____ rather than demolish the neighborhood.
   A. razing .. reanimate
   B. demolishing .. absolve
   C. annihilation .. exonerate
   D. obliteration .. exculpate
   E. censure .. vindicate

8. Vinnie was known for his _____ and cheerful disposition; he remained optimistic even when Eric and Ari were anxious about his career.
   A. angsty
   B. excruciating
   C. combustible
   D. sanguine
   E. incendiary

1. **C.** *Resolve* and *tenacity* mean *determination. Phantom* means *unseen, combustion* means *burning,* and *fusion* and *amalgamation* mean *coming together.*

2. **E.** *Berate* means *scold angrily,* so *censure* (formally denounce) is the best choice. *Combust* and *ignite* mean *burn,* and *annihilate* and *demolish* mean *destroy.*

3. **A.** *Sanguine* and *ebullient* mean *optimistic. Morose, doleful, lugubrious,* and *solemn* mean *serious and gloomy.*

4. **E.** *Raze* and *demolish* mean *destroy. Flog* means *whip;* and *admonish, censure,* and *chide* mean *scold angrily.*

5. **B.** "A surreptitious (secretive) person hopes to be phantom (unseen)."
   A. A clandestine (secretive) person hopes to be ebullient (optimistic) . . . no.
   B. A furtive (secretive) person hopes to be covert (secretive) . . . yes.
   C. A resolute (determined) person hopes to be excruciating (unbearable pain) . . . no.
   D. A sanguine (optimistic) person hopes to be incendiary (burning) . . . no.
   E. A buoyant (optimistic) person hopes to be pejorative (critical) . . . no.

6. **B.** "A pusillanimous (very shy) person lacks resolve (determination)."
   A. An incendiary (burnable) person lacks grit (resolve) . . . no.
   B. A very shy person lacks moxie (resolve) . . . yes.
   C. A very smart person lacks pertinacity (resolve) . . . no.
   D. A sanguine (optimistic) person lacks pluck (resolve) . . . no.
   E. An ebullient (optimistic) person lacks viscosity (thickness and stickiness) . . . no.

7. **A.** "In order to forestall the town's planned *demolishing* of the historic district, Akiko raised over $10,000 to help *not demolish* rather than demolish the neighborhood."

   Questions with two blanks are actually easier than questions with one blank—you have two opportunities to use the process of elimination. So, think of a word to fill each blank and then use the process of elimination, one blank at a time. *Raze* means *destroy,* and *reanimate* means *revive.*

8. **D.** "Vinnie was known for his *cheerful/optimistic* and cheerful disposition; he remained optimistic even when Eric and Ari were anxious about his career."

   Sanguine means *optimistic* and works best.

Celestial Dance

Find each of the following words on the *Breaking Dawn* page number provided. Based on the way each word is used in the book, guess at its definition.

1. **Filaments** (p. 387) might mean _____

   _____

2. **Motes** (p. 387) might mean _____

   _____

3. **Celestial** (p. 387) might mean _____

   _____

4. **Vortex** (p. 388) might mean _____

   _____

5. **Influx** (p. 388) might mean _____

   _____

6. **Stagnant** (p. 388) might mean _____

   _____

7. **Pyre** (p. 389) might mean _____

   _____

8. **Peripheral** (p. 389) might mean _____

   _____

Let's see how you did. Check your answers, write the exact definitions, and reread the sentence in *Breaking Dawn* where each word appears. Then complete the drills on the next page.

1. **Filaments** (p. 387) in this case means *thin wires inside a lightbulb that glow when heated*. *Filum* means *thread,* and *filaments* can actually refer to any *threads,* not just the ones in lightbulbs. I love this chapter in *Breaking Dawn;* you get to meet the newly transformed Bella, and you get your first glimpse inside the mind of a vampire—what Bella experiences, sees, hears, and feels . . . the filaments, the celestial dance of the dust motes, the eighth color of the light spectrum, the honey-lilac-and-sun-flavored scent, and the true appearance of Edward's face!

2. **Motes** (p. 387) means *tiny pieces of material.* Synonym: scintillas.

3. **Celestial** (p. 387) means *heavenly.* Remember from Group 17 that Atlas holds up the heavens, meaning the planets. *Celestial* can refer to *the planets* or to *the afterlife.* In this case, Bella means that the dust motes moved around each other like **planets** in orbit around the sun. Synonym: ethereal.

4. **Vortex** (p. 388) means *whirlpool.* Synonyms: eddy, maelstrom.

5. **Influx** (p. 388) means *large inflow.* Synonyms: deluge, incursion, inundation, torrent.

6. **Stagnant** (p. 388) means *still* or *stale.* Synonyms: dormant, lethargic, moribund, sluggish, static, stationary.

7. **Pyre** (p. 389) refers to *a structure on which a body is cremated (burned).* *Pyre* can also refer to the *heap of wood that fuels the fire.* Bella calls the table her "pyre" because during the transformation she felt like she was burning up.

8. **Peripheral** (p. 389) means *at the edge* (rather than at the center).

Synonyms: Select the word or phrase whose meaning is closest to the word in capital letters.

1. CELESTIAL
    A. ethereal
    B. peripheral
    C. dormant
    D. lethargic
    E. moribund

2. VORTEX
    A. filament
    B. mote
    C. scintilla
    D. maelstrom
    E. deluge

3. INFLUX
    A. pyre
    B. resolve
    C. inundation
    D. grit
    E. pluck

4. STAGNANT
    A. sanguine
    B. sluggish
    C. razed
    D. incendiary
    E. histrionic

Analogies: Select the answer choice that best completes the meaning of the sentence.

5. Stagnant is to movement as
    A. combustible is to pain
    B. sanguine is to negativity
    C. resolved is to determination
    D. aberrant is to fire
    E. viscous is to fusion

6. Vortex is to eddy as
    A. filament is to mote
    B. celestial is to ethereal
    C. influx is to stagnation
    D. torrent is to loathing
    E. pyre is to omnipresence

Sentence Completions: Choose the word or words that, when inserted in the sentence, best fits the meaning of the sentence as a whole.

7. Tia Dalma's fury unleashed a mighty _____, and the Flying Dutchman and the Black Pearl were forced to battle amid its swirling chaos.
    A. phantom
    B. aberration
    C. inferno
    D. tirade
    E. maelstrom

8. Each year a(n) _____ of tourists flock to the mountain resort; these many vacationers seek the fresh air of the mountain, hoping to leave behind the _____ city air.
    A. legion . . fresh
    B. horde . . cavernous
    C. incursion . . stagnant
    D. deluge . . somber
    E. periphery . . contumelious

1. **A.** *Celestial* and *ethereal* mean *heavenly. Peripheral* means *at the edge;* and *dormant, lethargic,* and *moribund* mean *stale.*
2. **D.** *Vortex* and *maelstrom* mean *whirlpool. Filament* means *thread, mote* and *scintilla* mean *tiny piece of material,* and *deluge* means *flood.*
3. **C.** *Influx* and *inundation* mean *inflow* or *flood. Pyre* means *place for cremation;* and *resolve, grit,* and *pluck* mean *determination.*
4. **B.** *Stagnant* means *sluggish. Sanguine* means *optimistic, razed* means *destroyed, incendiary* means *burnable,* and *histrionic* means *very dramatic.*
5. **B.** "Something stagnant lacks movement."
   A. Something combustible (burnable) lacks pain . . . no.
   B. Something sanguine (optimistic) lacks negativity . . . yes.
   C. Something resolved (determined) lacks determination . . . no.
   D. Something aberrant (abnormal) lacks fire . . . no.
   E. Something viscous (thick and gooey) lacks fusion (coming together) . . . no.
6. **B.** "Vortex (whirlpool) means the same thing as eddy (whirlpool)."
   A. Filament (thread) means the same thing as mote (speck) . . . no, both are small, but they are not synonyms.
   B. Celestial (heavenly) means the same thing as ethereal (heavenly) . . . yes.
   C. Influx (large inflow) means the same thing as stagnation (staleness) . . . no.
   D. Torrent (large inflow) means the same thing as loathing (hatred) . . . no.
   E. Pyre (place to cremate) means the same thing as omnipresence (all-knowingness) . . . no.
7. **E.** "Tia Dalma's fury unleashed a mighty <u>swirling chaos</u>, and the Flying Dutchman and the Black Pearl were forced to battle amid its swirling chaos."
   Maelstrom means *whirlpool* and fits perfectly. Base your answer **only** on evidence in the sentence. Tia Dalma might have unleashed a *phantom* (ghost), *aberration* (abnormality), *inferno* (massive fire), or *tirade* (angry speech), but you have evidence in the sentence **only** for "swirling chaos."
8. **C.** "Each year a(n) <u>lot</u> of tourists flock to the mountain resort; these many vacationers seek the fresh air of the mountain, hoping to leave behind the <u>not fresh</u> city air."
   Incursion means *large inflow,* and *stagnant* means *stale.*

New Vocabulary

Find each of the following words on the *Breaking Dawn* page number provided. Based on the way each word is used in the book, guess at its definition.

1. **Sideline** (p. 390) might mean _____

   _____

2. **Vocabulary** (p. 390) might mean _____

   _____

3. **Sinuously** (p. 391) might mean _____

   _____

4. **Fervor** (p. 396) might mean _____

   _____

5. **Devout** (p. 396) might mean _____

   _____

6. **Chagrin** (p. 397) might mean _____

   _____

7. **Pealing** (p. 398) might mean _____

   _____

8. **Infallible** (p. 398) might mean _____

   _____

Let's see how you did. Check your answers, write the exact definitions,
and reread the sentence in *Breaking Dawn* where each word appears.
Then complete the drills on the next page.

1. **Sideline** (p. 390) means *secondary (less important) thing*. This is
   a great example of a word that means exactly what it seems—
   something on the side, extra, less important. If you don't know a word,
   but can break it apart and have a hunch of what it means, go for it;
   you've probably got enough information to understand the gist of
   the word and get the question correct!

2. **Vocabulary** (p. 390) means *list of words*. You knew that already,
   but I included this word for three reasons. First, what you're
   holding is a **vocabulary** workbook. Second, *vocabulary* has great
   synonyms that you should learn. And third, and most important,
   Bella actually emphasizes the need for a large vocabulary, saying, "I
   gasped and then struggled with my vocabulary, unable to find the
   right words. I needed better words." Take it from Bella, you need
   to have a large vocabulary! Synonyms: lexicon, lexis.

3. **Sinuously** (p. 391) means *gracefully*. Synonyms for *sinuous*: agile,
   lissome, lithe, nimble, supple.

4. **Fervor** (p. 396) means *passion*. Synonyms: ardor, zeal.

5. **Devout** (p. 396) sounds like *devoted* and means, well, *devoted*.
   Synonyms: ardent, fervent, keen, pious, reverent, staunch,
   steadfast, sworn, unwavering, wholehearted, zealous.

6. **Chagrin** (p. 397) means *embarrassment*. Synonym: mortification.

7. **Pealing** (p. 398) means *reverberating ringing* and could be a
   synonym for *trilling* from Group 2. Both words are used to
   describe the sound of vampire speech or laughter. The synonyms
   for *trilling* were *quavering* and *warbling*. Two synonyms for
   peal are *carillon* and *tintinnabulation*. The first part of the word
   tintinnabulation even sounds like a bell ringing!

8. **Infallible** (p. 398) means *never failing*. Synonym: unerring.

Synonyms: Select the word or phrase whose meaning is closest to the word in capital letters.

1. VOCABULARY
   A. sideline
   B. chagrin
   C. lexicon
   D. mortification
   E. resolve

2. SINUOUS
   A. lithe
   B. pealing
   C. ardent
   D. zealous
   E. fervent

3. FERVOR
   A. infallibility
   B. ferocity
   C. dignity
   D. melodrama
   E. ardor

4. DEVOUT
   A. insouciant
   B. solicitous
   C. supercilious
   D. sanguine
   E. steadfast

Analogies: Select the answer choice that best completes the meaning of the sentence.

5. Infallible is to errors as
   A. pealing is to bells
   B. chagrined is to embarrassment
   C. fervor is to zeal
   D. sinuous is to awkwardness
   E. supple is to agility

6. Ardent is to sworn as
   A. keen is to pusillanimous
   B. steadfast is to haggard
   C. unwavering is to placating
   D. wholehearted is to pejorative
   E. zealous is to fervent

Sentence Completions: Choose the word that, when inserted in the sentence, <u>best</u> fits the meaning of the sentence as a whole.

7. Jacob noticed when Edward's attitude toward the fetus changed from fervent disdain to the opposite: staunch _____.
   A. chagrin
   B. lexis
   C. mandates
   D. devotion
   E. stagnancy

8. When Alex turned eight, his waning interest in chess changed from a devout passion to a _____ hobby.
   A. sinuous
   B. lissome
   C. sideline
   D. sworn
   E. wholehearted

1. **C.** *Vocabulary* and *lexicon* mean *list of words*. *Sideline* means *secondary,* *chagrin* and *mortification* mean *embarrassment,* and *resolve* means *determination.*

2. **A.** *Sinuous* and *lithe* mean *graceful*. *Pealing* means *ringing;* and *ardent, zealous,* and *fervent* mean *passionate.*

3. **E.** *Fervor* and *ardor* mean *passion*. *Infallibility* means *not making errors, ferocity* means *intensity,* and *melodrama* means *drama.*

4. **E.** *Devout* and *steadfast* mean *devoted*. Use the process of elimination—cross off answers that you are **sure** don't work and choose the best of what's left. *Insouciant* means *uncaring, solicitous* means *caring, supercilious* means *arrogant, sanguine* means *optimistic.*

5. **D.** "Infallible means without errors."
   - A. Pealing (ringing) means without bells . . . no.
   - B. Chagrined (embarrassed) means without embarrassment . . . no.
   - C. Fervor (passion) means without zeal (passion) . . . no.
   - (D.) Sinuous (graceful) means without awkwardness . . . yes.
   - E. Supple (graceful) means without agility (grace) . . . no.

6. **E.** "Ardent (devoted) means the same thing as sworn."
   - A. Keen (devoted) means the same thing as pusillanimous (very shy) . . . no.
   - B. Steadfast (devoted) means the same thing as haggard (unhealthy-looking) . . . no.
   - C. Unwavering (devoted) means the same thing as placating (soothing) . . . no.
   - D. Wholehearted (devoted) means the same thing as pejorative (critical) . . . no.
   - (E.) Zealous (devoted) means the same thing as fervent (devoted) . . . yes.

7. **D.** "Jacob noticed when Edward's attitude toward the fetus changed from fervent disdain to the opposite: staunch *not disdain/love*."
   Devotion means *love* or *loyalty* and fits best.

8. **C.** "When Alex turned eight, his waning interest in chess changed from a devout passion to a *not devout* hobby."
   Sideline means *secondary* and fits better than the other choices. Even if you did not know the word *waning* (lessening), you could still get this question correct. When you don't know a word in the sentence, try answering without it. Often you can still determine what is needed for the blank—since Alex's interest **changed,** his "_____ hobby" must be different than "devout passion."

Quiz 4

I. Let's review some of the words that you've seen in Groups 16–20. Match each of the following words to the correct definition or synonym on the right. Then check the solutions on page 171.

1.	Eventuality	A.	Censure
2.	Condemn	B.	Gelatinous
3.	Absolve	C.	Ebullient
4.	Congealing	D.	Contingency
5.	Viscous	E.	Dormant
6.	Aberration	F.	Exonerate
7.	Resolve	G.	Amalgamating
8.	Sanguine	H.	Lexicon
9.	Raze	I.	Deluge
10.	Vortex	J.	Anomaly
11.	Influx	K.	Tenacity
12.	Stagnant	L.	Eddy
13.	Vocabulary	M.	Demolish
14.	Sinuous	N.	Ardor
15.	Fervor	O.	Lithe

II. Let's review several of the word parts that you've seen in Groups 16–20. Match each of the following word parts to the correct definition or synonym on the right. Then check the solutions on page 171.

16.	Hyper-	A.	Together
17.	Con-	B.	Before or much
18.	Re-	C.	Very
19.	Filum-	D.	Same
20.	Pro-	E.	Thread
21.	Homo-	F.	Again

Review

Match each group of synonyms to its general meaning. Then check the solutions on page 171.

1. Absolve
   Acquit
   Exculpate
   Exonerate
   Pardon
   Vindicate

   A. Passionate

2. Ardent
   Fervent
   Fervid
   Keen
   Zealous

   B. Graceful

3. Aberration
   Anomaly
   Deviation
   Divergence
   Perversion

   C. Whirlpool

4. Buoyant
   Ebullient
   Sanguine

   D. Optimistic and cheerful

5. Agile
   Lissome
   Lithe
   Nimble
   Sinuous
   Supple

   E. Abnormality

6. Eddy
   Maelstrom
   Vortex

   F. Free of blame

Group 21
Innovative Injection

Find each of the following words on the *Breaking Dawn* page number provided. Based on the way each word is used in the book, guess at its definition.

1. **Animosity** (p. 400) might mean _____

    _____

2. **Innovative** (p. 400) might mean _____

    _____

3. **Voyeuristic** (p. 403) might mean _____

    _____

4. **Gratification** (p. 403) might mean _____

    _____

5. **Luminous** (p. 403) might mean _____

    _____

6. **Presage** (p. 404) might mean _____

    _____

7. **Verdict** (p. 404) might mean _____

    _____

8. **Exultant** (p. 413) might mean _____

    _____

Let's see how you did. Check your answers, write the exact definitions,
and reread the sentence in *Breaking Dawn* where each word appears.
Then complete the drills on the next page.

1. **Animosity** (p. 400) means *hostility* or even *hatred*. Synonyms: acrimony, antipathy, enmity, rancor. *Antipathy* is an interesting word to break apart. *Anti-* means *against*, and *path-* refers to *feeling*, as in *empathy* (sharing another's **feelings**), so *antipathy* means *feeling against—hostility*.

2. **Innovative** (p. 400) means *new and original*. This reminds me of a hilarious scene in *Old School* when Will Ferrell's character competes in the debate portion of his fraternity's charter review. The Dean asks a ridiculously difficult debate question ("What is your position on the role of government in supporting **innovation** in the field of biotechnology?") to which Will Ferrell's character gives an uncharacteristically brilliant answer before grunting and falling limp on the podium. Synonyms: avant-garde, groundbreaking, novel, pioneering, unprecedented.

3. **Voyeuristic** (p. 403) means *deriving enjoyment from watching others* and comes from the French word *voir* for *see*.

4. **Gratification** (p. 403) means *enjoyment*. Synonym: indulgence.

5. **Luminous** (p. 403) means *radiant* or *shedding light*. *Lumin-* means *light*, as in *luminary* (a person who "sheds light" and inspires others) and *Lumos*, the spell in the *Harry Potter* books and movies that causes a caster's wand to **shed light** like a flashlight.

6. **Presage** (p. 404) means *warn of something bad*. *Pre-* means *before*, and *sage* means *understand*, so *understand before—warn*. Synonyms: augur, forebode, foreshadow, foretell, portend, prophesy.

7. **Verdict** (p. 404) means *ruling* or *judgment*. Synonym: adjudication.

8. **Exultant** (p. 413) means *thrilled*. Synonyms: buoyant, ebullient, ecstatic, elated, euphoric, exuberant, jubilant, rapturous.

Synonyms: Select the word or phrase whose meaning is closest to the word in capital letters.

1. ANIMOSITY
   A. enmity
   B. chagrin
   C. vortex
   D. eddy
   E. maelstrom

2. GRATIFICATION
   A. resolve
   B. grit
   C. moxie
   D. pertinacity
   E. indulgence

3. PRESAGE
   A. raze
   B. annihilate
   C. augur
   D. censure
   E. reproof

4. EXULTANT
   A. luminous
   B. elated
   C. voyeuristic
   D. innovative
   E. unerring

Analogies: Select the answer choice that best completes the meaning of the sentence.

5. Exultant is to lugubrious as
   A. buoyant is to luminous
   B. ebullient is to voyeuristic
   C. ecstatic is to doleful
   D. avant-garde is to gloomy
   E. novel is to somber

6. Judge is to verdict as
   A. vampire is to presage
   B. Volturi is to lexicon
   C. teacher is to deluge
   D. werewolf is to torrent
   E. principal is to adjudication

Sentence Completions: Choose the word or words that, when inserted in the sentence, <u>best</u> fits the meaning of the sentence as a whole.

7. The _____ technology of nuclear science is totally new, yet philosophers and scientists _____ its development many years ago.
   A. acrimonious .. presaged
   B. innovative .. obliterated
   C. groundbreaking .. augured
   D. histrionic .. portended
   E. pioneering .. flogged

8. Rachel was outraged to witness the prevalence of poverty and inequality around the world and her _____ for injustice as well as her plan to fight it deepened.
   A. enmity
   B. gratification
   C. chagrin
   D. fervor
   E. ardor

1. **A.** *Animosity* and *enmity* mean *hostility. Chagrin* means *embarrassment;* and *vortex, eddy,* and *maelstrom* mean *whirlpool.*

2. **E.** *Gratification* and *indulgence* mean *enjoyment. Resolve, grit, moxie,* and *pertinacity* mean *determination.*

3. **C.** *Presage* and *augur* mean *predict. Raze* and *annihilate* mean *destroy,* and *censure* and *reproof* mean *scold severely.*

4. **B.** *Exultant* and *elated* mean *thrilled. Luminous* means *shedding light, voyeuristic* means *enjoying watching others, innovative* means *new and original,* and *unerring* means *never failing.*

5. **C.** "Exultant (thrilled) is the opposite of lugubrious (gloomy)."
   A. Buoyant (thrilled) is the opposite of luminous (shedding light) . . . no.
   B. Ebullient (thrilled) is the opposite of voyeuristic (enjoying watching others) . . . no.
   C. Ecstatic (thrilled) is the opposite of doleful (gloomy) . . . yes.
   D. Avant-garde (new and original) is the opposite of gloomy . . . no.
   E. Novel (new and original) is the opposite of somber (gloomy) . . . no.

6. **E.** "A judge gives a verdict (judgment)."
   A. A vampire gives a presage (warning) . . . no, not most vampires, only Alice.
   B. A Volturi gives a lexicon (list of words) . . . no.
   C. A teacher gives a deluge (flood) . . . no.
   D. A werewolf gives a torrent (flood) . . . no.
   E. A principal gives an adjudication (punishment) . . . maybe. Choice E is the best answer.

7. **C.** "The _new_ technology of nuclear science is totally new, yet philosophers and scientists _????_ its development many years ago."
   Use the process of elimination one blank at a time, and make sure your answer choice fits the evidence in the sentence. *Groundbreaking* means *new,* and *augured* means *predicted. Acrimonious* means *hostile,* and *histrionic* means *dramatic.*

8. **A.** "Rachel was outraged to witness the prevalence of poverty and inequality around the world and her _outrage_ for injustice as well as her plan to fight it deepened."
   Enmity means *hostility* and works best with the evidence "outraged."

Group 22
Feral Snarl

Find each of the following words on the *Breaking Dawn* page number provided. Based on the way each word is used in the book, guess at its definition.

1. **Mutiny** (p. 414) might mean _____

   _____

2. **Desiccated** (p. 416) might mean _____

   _____

3. **Compulsory** (p. 417) might mean _____

   _____

4. **Feral** (p. 417) might mean _____

   _____

5. **Deprivation** (p. 418) might mean _____

   _____

6. **Blasphemy** (p. 419) might mean _____

   _____

7. **Resin** (p. 421) might mean _____

   _____

8. **Tawny** (p. 422) might mean _____

   _____

Let's see how you did. Check your answers, write the exact definitions,
and reread the sentence in *Breaking Dawn* where each word appears.
Then complete the drills on the next page.

1. **Mutiny** (p. 414) means *rebellion*. Bella was enjoying running,
   and particularly enjoying running faster than Edward, so when
   he called for her to stop, she considered **rebellion**. *Mutiny* is
   most often used to indicate **rebellion** *against a captain on a ship*,
   so you hear this word often in the *Pirates of the Caribbean* movies.
   Synonyms: insubordination, insurgence, insurrection, uprising.

2. **Desiccated** (p. 416) means *very dry*. Synonyms: arid, dehydrated,
   parched, sere. Those odd little packages that you find with new
   leather shoes and vitamins to help keep things dry are called
   desiccants.

3. **Compulsory** (p. 417) means *required,* as Bella says, "there wasn't
   a choice." Synonyms: mandatory, obligatory (like the word
   obligation), requisite.

4. **Feral** (p. 417) means *wild or ferocious*. Synonyms: savage,
   undomesticated. Can you believe she snarled at Edward?! Still,
   Bella's self-control in this scene is amazing!

5. **Deprivation** (p. 418) means *lack of*. Holding her breath (and
   therefore not getting new scents) gave Bella **sensory deprivation**
   since the sense of smell is so primary for vampires.

6. **Blasphemy** (p. 419) is the opposite of *reverence* and means
   disrespect for sacred things. Synonyms: desecration, execration,
   impiety, irreverence, profanity, sacrilege.

7. **Resin** (p. 421) refers to *a gummy substance secreted by trees*. Resin is
   the sticky stuff you sometimes get on your hand when you handle
   a pinecone. It is used in skateboards, bowling balls, and for violin
   bows. Bella refers to the scent of "pitch and resin." *Pitch* is similar
   to resin, but can also come from petroleum rather than only from
   plants, so it's more tar-like than resin. Stephenie Meyer has a
   seriously good vocabulary!

8. **Tawny** (p. 422) sounds a bit like *tan* and means *yellowish-brown*.
   Synonym: fulvous.

Synonyms: Select the word or phrase whose meaning is closest to the word in capital letters.

1. MUTINY
   A. deprivation
   B. insurgence
   C. animosity
   D. acrimony
   E. antipathy

2. DESICCATED
   A. arid
   B. feral
   C. tawny
   D. fulvous
   E. novel

3. COMPULSORY
   A. buoyant
   B. ebullient
   C. euphoric
   D. jubilant
   E. requisite

4. BLASPHEMY
   A. resin
   B. pitch
   C. insurrection
   D. impiety
   E. zeal

Analogies: Select the answer choice that best completes the meaning of the sentence.

5. Resin is to trees as
   A. guffaw is to incubus
   B. horde is to eventuality
   C. trepidation is to chaos
   D. loam is to ground
   E. belfry is to bats

6. Mutiny is to desiccated as
   A. compulsory is to dehydrated
   B. feral is to sere
   C. deprivation is to parched
   D. insurrection is to arid
   E. blasphemy is to desecration

Sentence Completions: Choose the word that, when inserted in the sentence, best fits the meaning of the sentence as a whole.

7. Attendance at all meetings of the club was _____ for members in good standing, and even one absence could result in a suspended membership.
   A. arid
   B. obligatory
   C. blasphemous
   D. fulvous
   E. sanguine

8. Matty hoped to free himself from the confines of society and unleash the more _____ side of his personality.
   A. feral
   B. exultant
   C. presaged
   D. rancorous
   E. voyeuristic

1. **B.** *Mutiny* and *insurgence* mean *rebellion. Deprivation* means *lack of;* and *animosity, acrimony,* and *antipathy* mean *hostility,* which might cause a rebellion, but *insurgence* is a much more direct synonym for *mutiny.*

2. **A.** *Desiccated* and *arid* mean *very dry. Feral* means *wild, tawny* and *fulvous* mean *yellowish-brown,* and *novel* means *new and original.*

3. **E.** *Compulsory* and *requisite* mean *required. Buoyant, ebullient, euphoric,* and *jubilant* mean *thrilled.*

4. **D.** *Blasphemy* and *impiety* mean *disrespect for sacred things.* In fact, *im-* means *not,* and *piety* means *religious respect,* so *impiety* means *not religious respect. Resin* and *pitch* are *gummy substances, insurrection* means *rebellion,* and *zeal* means *passion. Insurrection* might be considered a type of *blasphemy,* but *impiety* is a more direct synonym.

5. **D.** "Resin comes from trees."
   A. Guffaw (hearty laugh) comes from an incubus (male demon) . . . no.
   B. Horde (mob) comes from an eventuality (possibility) . . . no.
   C. Trepidation (fear) comes from chaos (disorder) . . . no.
   (D.) Loam (rich soil) comes from the ground . . . yes.
   E. Belfry (bell tower) comes from bats . . . no.

6. **D.** "Mutiny (rebellion) is to desiccated (very dry)."
   When the words in the question are completely unrelated, they are probably related to the words below.
   A. Compulsory (required) is to dehydrated (very dry) . . . no.
   B. Feral (wild) is to sere (very dry) . . . no.
   C. Deprivation (lack of) is to parched (very dry) . . . no.
   (D.) Insurrection (rebellion) is to arid (very dry) . . . yes.
   E. Blasphemy (disrespect for sacred things) is to desecration (disrespect for sacred things) . . . no.
   Choice D is best; *mutiny* means the same thing as *insurrection,* and *desiccated* means the same thing as *arid.*

7. **B.** "Attendance at all meetings of the club was <u>required</u> for members in good standing, and even one absence could result in a suspended membership."
   Use the process of elimination. *Obligatory* means *required.*

8. **A.** "Matty hoped to free himself from the confines of society and unleash the more <u>unconfined</u> side of his personality."
   Look for evidence. Matty may have hoped to unleash the *exultant* (thrilled), *presaged* (predicted), *rancorous* (hostile), or even *voyeuristic* (enjoying watching others) side of his personality, but you have evidence **only** that he was freeing "himself from the confines of society," so *feral* (wild) fits best.

Herbivore?

Find each of the following words on the *Breaking Dawn* page number provided. Based on the way each word is used in the book, guess at its definition.

1. **Purchase** (p. 422) might mean _____

_____

2. **Feeble** (p. 422) might mean _____

_____

3. **Sinews** (p. 422) might mean _____

_____

4. **In tatters** (p. 423) might mean _____

_____

5. **Herbivores** (p. 424) might mean _____

_____

6. **Averse to** (p. 427) might mean _____

_____

7. **Aura** (p. 427) might mean _____

_____

8. **Rueful** (p. 427) might mean _____

_____

Let's see how you did. Check your answers, write the exact definitions, and reread the sentence in *Breaking Dawn* where each word appears. Then complete the drills on the next page.

1. **Purchase** (p. 422) in this case means *grip*. It can also, of course, refer to *something bought*, but the context on page 422 in *Breaking Dawn* tells you that it means *grip*. The SAT, ACT, GED, and SSAT love to use a word like this that has several meanings and ask you to determine its meaning in context. Bella explains that the huge mountain lion was powerless against her and that its "teeth could find no purchase against my shoulder." She's saying that even a giant mountain lion could not bite her!

2. **Feeble** (p. 422) means *very weak*. Synonym: frail.

3. **Sinews** (p. 422) means *tendons and ligaments*. Sorry if this grosses you out, but hey, Bella's got to eat.

4. **In tatters** (p. 423) means *in shreds*. Synonym: threadbare.

5. **Herbivores** (p. 424) means *plant-eaters—vegetarians*, as opposed to *carnivores* (meat-eaters) or *omnivores* (meat- and vegetable-eaters). Lots of terrific word parts here. *Herb* means *plant*, *carn-* means *flesh*, *omni-* means *all*, and *-vore* comes from the Latin word *vorare*, meaning *swallow*. So you have the *plant swallowers*, the *meat swallowers*, and the *everything swallowers*.

6. **Averse to** (p. 427) means *against*. Don't confuse *averse* with *adverse*, which means *unfavorable*, as in *Edward was originally **averse to** (against) Bella's pregnancy because he feared that it would have drastically **adverse** (unfavorable) effects on Bella's health*. The two words are related (*against* is similar to *unfavorable*), but *averse* applies to attitudes, and *adverse* applies to situations.

7. **Aura** (p. 427) means *atmosphere*.

8. **Rueful** (p. 427) means *regretful*. In *Shrek 2*, Prince Charming waves his sword shouting, "He will rue the very day he stole my kingdom . . . " just as a bird poops on him (DreamWorks, 2004). He is saying that Shrek will **regret** stealing the kingdom. Synonyms: contrite, penitent, remorseful, repentant.

Synonyms: Select the word or phrase whose meaning is closest to the word in capital letters.

1. FEEBLE
   A. penitent
   B. repentant
   C. tawny
   D. fulvous
   E. frail

2. IN TATTERS
   A. threadbare
   B. desiccated
   C. compulsory
   D. feral
   E. euphoric

3. AVERSE TO
   A. herbivorous
   B. omnivorous
   C. against
   D. carnivorous
   E. unerring

4. RUEFUL
   A. ardent
   B. fervent
   C. keen
   D. contrite
   E. steadfast

Analogies: Select the answer choice that best completes the meaning of the sentence.

5. Herbivores are to plants as
   A. vampires are to werewolves
   B. carnivores are to sinews
   C. omnivores are to auras
   D. goats are to chagrin
   E. Renesmee is to tatters

6. Feeble is to strong as
   A. prosaic is to pedestrian
   B. analogous is to commensurate
   C. homologous is to corresponding
   D. premeditation is to haste
   E. sallow is to wan

Sentence Completions: Choose the word that, when inserted in the sentence, <u>best</u> fits the meaning of the sentence as a whole.

7. No matter how hard she tried to grasp his motivations, Liz could find no _____ on Jack's reasons for adding Tracy to the show.
   A. contrition
   B. purchase
   C. aura
   D. deprivation
   E. impiety

8. Jenna was so fond of her _____, old jacket that she had it made into a quilt after it was no longer usable as a coat.
   A. rueful
   B. sanguine
   C. histrionic
   D. omniscient
   E. threadbare

1. **E.** *Feeble* and *frail* mean *very weak*. *Penitent* and *repentant* mean *regretful*, and *tawny* and *fulvous* mean *yellowish-brown*.
2. **A.** *In tatters* and *threadbare* mean *in shreds*. *Desiccated* means *very dry*, *compulsory* means *required*, *feral* means *wild*, and *euphoric* means *thrilled*.
3. **C.** *Averse to* means *against*. *Herbivorous* means *plant-eating*, *omnivorous* means *everything-eating*, *carnivorous* means *meat-eating*, and *unerring* means *not making errors*.
4. **D.** *Rueful* and *contrite* mean *regretful*. *Ardent*, *fervent*, *keen*, and *steadfast* mean *devoted*.
5. **B.** "Herbivores eat plants."
   - A. Vampires eat werewolves . . . no, they may fight them, but they definitely don't eat them.
   - (B.) Carnivores (meat-eaters) eat sinews (tendons and ligaments) . . . yes.
   - C. Omnivores (everything-eaters) eat auras (atmospheres) . . . no.
   - D. Goats eat chagrin (embarrassment) . . . no.
   - E. Renesmee eats tatters (shreds) . . . no, though she may like taters (potatoes) since she can eat like a human or a vampire.
6. **D.** "Feeble (very weak) is the opposite of strong."
   - A. Prosaic (ordinary and unimaginative) is the opposite of pedestrian (ordinary and unimaginative) . . . no.
   - B. Analogous (matching) is the opposite of commensurate (matching) . . . no.
   - C. Homologous (matching) is the opposite of corresponding (matching) . . . no.
   - (D.) Premeditation (planning) is the opposite of haste (rushing) . . . yes.
   - E. Sallow (pale) is the opposite of wan (pale) . . . no.
7. **B.** "No matter how hard she tried to grasp his motivations, Liz could find no <u>grasp</u> on Jack's reasons for adding Tracy to the show."

   Purchase can mean *grip* and fits best.
8. **D.** "Jenna was so fond of her <u>old,</u> old jacket that she had it made into a quilt after it was no longer usable as a coat."

   Think of a word you'd like to see, taking a word or words right from the sentence when possible and then use the process of elimination. *Threadbare* means *shredded* and fits best. *Rueful* means *regretful*, *sanguine* means *optimistic*, *histrionic* means *dramatic*, and *omniscient* means *all-knowing*.

Group 24
Unnecessary Rebukes

Find each of the following words on the *Breaking Dawn* page number provided. Based on the way each word is used in the book, guess at its definition.

1. **Indignation** (p. 430) might mean _____

_____

2. **Bodice** (p. 431) might mean _____

_____

3. **Intact** (p. 433) might mean _____

_____

4. **Theatrically** (p. 436) might mean _____

_____

5. **Proximity** (p. 438) might mean _____

_____

6. **Chided** (p. 439) might mean _____

_____

7. **Chastened** (p. 441) might mean _____

_____

8. **Rebuke** (p. 441) might mean _____

_____

Let's see how you did. Check your answers, write the exact definitions, 99
and reread the sentence in *Breaking Dawn* where each word appears.
Then complete the drills on the next page.

1. **Indignation** (p. 430) means *anger or resentment about unfair treatment.* Synonyms: affront, ire, pique, umbrage, vexation. The word *umbrage* makes me think of the very **angry, resentful,** and generally nasty character, Dolores **Umbridge,** who takes over Hogwarts in *Harry Potter and the Order of the Phoenix.*

2. **Bodice** (p. 431) sounds like *body* and refers to *the part of a dress above the waist.* This is a pretty fancy word, and you've got to appreciate Stephenie Meyer's vocab again here. *Bodice,* which is also a piece of clothing, makes me think of the equally unusual word *raiment,* meaning *clothing,* which I saw recently on an SAT.

3. **Intact** (p. 433) means *complete and undamaged.* Bella describes the word in the sentence that follows it, "It was just like before"— *undamaged.* Notice how often you can figure out the meaning of a word from the context. *Intact* is also an interesting word to break apart. *In-* means *not,* and *tact-* refers to *touch,* as in *tactile* (which actually means *relating to the sense of touch*), so *intact* means *not touched—undamaged.* Synonyms: inviolate, pristine, undefiled, unimpaired, unscathed, unsullied.

4. **Theatrically** (p. 436) means *very dramatically* and reminds me of *melodramatic* and its synonyms, *histrionic* and *operatic* from Group 15.

5. **Proximity** (p. 438) means *nearness,* like in *High School Musical* when Ms. Darbus punishes Bolton by forcing him to help out in the theater and saying "**proximity** to the arts is cleansing for the soul." (Disney, 2006) Synonym: propinquity.

6. **Chided** (p. 439) means *scolded* and was a synonym for *berated* in Group 18. The other synonyms were *admonished, censured, rebuked, reprimanded, reproached,* and *reproved.* Another great synonym that you might see on standardized tests is *remonstrated.*

7. **Chastened** (p. 441) is similar to *chided* but means *disciplined.* Even though Edward is almost a hundred years old, Carlisle is still a discipline-dispensing Dad; I hope Edward does not get grounded. ☺

8. **Rebuke** (p. 441) is another word for *scold.* Everyone is on edge and **scolding** each other as newborn Bella is about to meet Renesmee.

Synonyms: Select the word or phrase whose meaning is closest to the word in capital letters.

1. INDIGNATION
   A. bodice
   B. raiment
   C. purchase
   D. umbrage
   E. desecration

2. INTACT
   A. theatrical
   B. pristine
   C. histrionic
   D. operatic
   E. chastened

3. PROXIMITY
   A. resin
   B. insurgence
   C. adjudication
   D. inundation
   E. propinquity

4. CHIDE
   A. rebuke
   B. presage
   C. augur
   D. forebode
   E. portend

Analogies: Select the answer choice that best completes the meaning of the sentence.

5. Bodice is to raiment as
   A. aberration is to normality
   B. resolve is to scolding
   C. lexicon is to fervor
   D. exultant is to mood
   E. arid is to uprising

6. Censure is to reprove as
   A. chide is to absolve
   B. admonish is to reprimand
   C. rebuke is to acquit
   D. chasten is to exonerate
   E. rue to prevaricate

Sentence Completions: Choose the word that, when inserted in the sentence, <u>best</u> fits the meaning of the sentence as a whole.

7. Jasper feared that _____ to Renesmee would be too much temptation for Bella to handle, so he tried to keep them a good distance apart.
   A. synchronization
   B. propinquity
   C. animosity
   D. acrimony
   E. enmity

8. Diego was _____ when his friends thoughtlessly left him without a ride home.
   A. piqued
   B. intact
   C. omnivorous
   D. arid
   E. elated

1. **D.** *Indignation* and *umbrage* mean *resentment. Bodice* means the *part*
of a dress above the waste, raiment means *clothing, purchase* means
grip, and *desecration* means *disrespect of something sacred.*
2. **B.** *Intact* and *pristine* mean *undamaged. Theatrical, histrionic,* and
operatic mean *very dramatic;* and *chastened* means *disciplined.*
3. **E.** *Proximity* and *propinquity* mean *nearness. Resin* means *sticky
secretion from a tree, insurgence* means *rebellion, adjudication* means
official judgment, and *inundation* means *flood.*
4. **A.** *Chide* and *rebuke* both mean *scold. Presage, augur, forebode,* and
portend mean *predict.*
5. **D.** "Bodice (the part of a dress above the waste) is a type of
raiment (clothing)."
   A. Aberration (abnormality) is a type of normality . . . no.
   B. Resolve (determination) is a type of scolding . . . no.
   C. Lexicon (list of words) is a type of fervor (passion) . . . no.
   D. Exultant (thrilled) is a type of mood . . . yes.
   E. Arid (very dry) is a type of uprising (rebellion) . . . no.
6. **B.** "Censure (scold) is a synonym of reprove."
   A. Chide (scold) is a synonym of absolve (clear of blame) . . . no.
   B. Admonish (scold) is a synonym of reprimand (scold) . . . yes.
   C. Rebuke (scold) is a synonym of acquit (clear of blame) . . . no.
   D. Chasten (discipline) is a synonym of exonerate (clear of
      blame) . . . no.
   E. Rue (regret) is a synonym of prevaricate (avoid) . . . no.
7. **B.** "Jasper feared that _not a good distance_ to Renesmee would be
   too much temptation for Bella to handle, so he tried to keep
   them a good distance apart."

   If you can't come up with a word for the blank, use the
   process of elimination. Eliminate choices **only** when you are
   absolutely positive that they don't fit, and then choose the best
   of the remaining choices. *Propinquity* means *nearness* and fits the
   evidence of the sentence best.
8. **A.** "Diego was _upset_ when his friends thoughtlessly left him
   without a ride home."

   Piqued means *resentful* and best fits the evidence that Diego's
   friends "thoughtlessly left him without a ride."

Group 25
Petulant Newborn

Find each of the following words on the *Breaking Dawn* page number provided. Based on the way each word is used in the book, guess at its definition.

1. **Boggling** (p. 446) might mean _____

_____

2. **Rhetorically** (p. 446) might mean _____

_____

3. **Mitigated** (p. 452) might mean _____

_____

4. **Articulated** (p. 453) might mean _____

_____

5. **Petulant** (p. 454) might mean _____

_____

6. **Antagonistic** (p. 455) might mean _____

_____

7. **Unobtrusively** (p. 455) might mean _____

_____

8. **Newel** (p. 455) might mean _____

_____

Let's see how you did. Check your answers, write the exact definitions, and reread the sentence in *Breaking Dawn* where each word appears. Then complete the drills on the next page.

1. **Boggling** (p. 446) in this case means *staggered and astonished.* Interestingly, *boggling* comes from *bogey,* meaning *a troublesome phantom* or, more generally, *something that staggers,* and makes me think of boggarts, in the *Harry Potter* books, which take on the shape of a victim's worst fear and are pretty **staggering** (unless you cast a *Riddikulus spell,* which makes the boggarts look ridiculous rather than staggering).

2. **Rhetorically** (p. 446) in this case means *with no answer expected.* It can also refer to *the stylistic and effective use of language,* and in fact, the SAT often uses the word *rhetoric* to mean *style, versus substance.*

3. **Mitigated** (p. 452) means *lessened* or *soothed.* Synonyms: abated, allayed, alleviated, ameliorated, appeased, assuaged, attenuated, conciliated, mollified, pacified, palliated, placated, propitiated, tempered.

4. **Articulated** (p. 453) means *clearly pronounced.* Every time Bella begins to apologize, someone cuts her off and tells her that she's doing great as a newborn vampire. Because they keep cutting her off, she hasn't gotten out "a fully **articulated** apology."

5. **Petulant** (p. 454) means *irritable.* Synonyms: cantankerous, churlish, curmudgeonly, fractious, irascible, peevish, querulous, sullen. *Querulous* is easy to remember because it sounds like having a *quarrel* (angry disagreement).

6. **Antagonistic** (p. 455) means *hostile.* Synonyms: bellicose, belligerent, oppugnant, pugnacious, truculent.

7. **Unobtrusively** (p. 455) means *discreetly.* Synonyms: circumspectly, inconspicuously. This is also a great place to review the related word *furtively* (secretly) and its synonyms *clandestinely, covertly,* and *surreptitiously* for Group 4.

8. **Newel** (p. 455) refers to *the post at the beginning or end of a stairway handrail.*

Synonyms: Select the word or phrase whose meaning is closest to the word in capital letters.

Drills

1. RHETORIC
   A. newel
   B. style
   C. bodice
   D. raiment
   E. proximity

2. MITIGATE
   A. articulate
   B. mollify
   C. boggle
   D. reprove
   E. censure

3. PETULANT
   A. unobtrusive
   B. surreptitious
   C. furtive
   D. churlish
   E. clandestine

4. ANTAGONISTIC
   A. assuaged
   B. ameliorated
   C. conciliated
   D. tempered
   E. truculent

Analogies: Select the answer choice that best completes the meaning of the sentence.

5. Mitigate is to worsen as
   A. abate is to rectify
   B. allay is to redress
   C. alleviate is to deteriorate
   D. appease is to boggle
   E. palliate is to indemnify

6. Newel is to stairway as
   A. intermission is to play
   B. histrionic is to theater
   C. loam is to soil
   D. prelude is to conclusion
   E. overture is to opera

Sentence Completions: Choose the word or words that, when inserted in the sentence, best fits the meaning of the sentence as a whole.

7. Francis stalked _____ past the front line hoping to avoid notice from the _____ enemy troops.
   A. unobtrusively .. articulated
   B. furtively .. tempered
   C. operatically .. petulant
   D. clandestinely .. intact
   E. surreptitiously .. belligerent

8. Andrew hoped that his careful articulation would be an effective _____ device that would cause the audience to listen closely and grasp the gravity of his topic.
   A. boggling
   B. mitigating
   C. querulous
   D. rhetorical
   E. contrite

1. **B.** *Rhetoric* means *style. Newel* refers to *the railing post at the beginning or end of a stairway, bodice* means *upper part of a dress, raiment* means *clothing,* and *proximity* mean *nearness.*

2. **B.** *Mitigate* and *mollify* mean *lessen* or *soothe. Articulate* means *express clearly, boggle* mean *stagger,* and *reprove* and *censure* mean *scold strongly.*

3. **D.** *Petulant* and *churlish* mean *irritable. Unobtrusive, surreptitious, furtive,* and *clandestine* mean *secret.*

4. **E.** *Antagonistic* and *truculent* mean *hostile. Assuaged, ameliorated, conciliated,* and *tempered* mean *lessened* or *soothed.*

5. **C.** "Mitigate (lessen, soothe) is the opposite of worsen."
   A. Abate (lessen, soothe) is the opposite of rectify (make up for) . . . no.
   B. Allay (lessen, soothe) is the opposite of redress (make up for) . . . no.
   C. Alleviate (lessen, soothe) is the opposite of deteriorate . . . yes.
   D. Appease (lessen, soothe) is the opposite of boggle (stagger) . . . no.
   E. Palliate (lessen, soothe) is the opposite of indemnify (make up for) . . . no.

6. **E.** "A newel is at the beginning of a stairway."
   A. An intermission is at the beginning of a play . . . no.
   B. A histrionic (dramatic) is at the beginning of a theater . . . no.
   C. A loam (soil) is at the beginning of a soil . . . no.
   D. A prelude (introduction) is at the beginning of a conclusion . . . no.
   E. An overture (introduction) is at the beginning of an opera . . . yes.

7. **E.** "Francis stalked *hoping to avoid notice* past the front line hoping to avoid notice from the *enemy* enemy troops."
   Use the process of elimination one blank at a time. *Surreptitiously* means *secretly,* and *belligerent* means *hostile.*

8. **D.** "Andrew hoped that his careful articulation would be an effective *????* device that would cause the audience to listen closely and grasp the gravity of his topic."
   Rhetorical means *stylistic* and fits best. Use evidence in the sentence to choose your answer. Andrew used **style** (careful articulation) to convey his meaning to the audience.

Quiz 5

I. Let's review some of the words that you've seen in Groups 21–25. Match each of the following words to the correct definition or synonym on the right. Then check the solutions on page 172.

1. Animosity	A. Augur
2. Presage	B. Frail
3. Exultant	C. Acrimony
4. Mutiny	D. Arid
5. Desiccated	E. Jubilant
6. Blasphemy	F. Contrite
7. Feeble	G. Ameliorate
8. In tatters	H. Insurgence
9. Rueful	I. Histrionic
10. Indignation	J. Impiety
11. Intact	K. Threadbare
12. Theatrical	L. Irascible
13. Rhetorical	M. Inviolate
14. Mitigate	N. Umbrage
15. Petulant	O. Stylistic

II. Let's review several of the word parts that you've seen in Groups 21–25. Match each of the following word parts to the correct definition or synonym on the right. Then check the solutions on page 172.

16. Anti-	A. Light
17. Carn-	B. Touch
18. Omni-	C. Against
19. Path-	D. Feeling
20. Tact-	E. All
21. Lumin-	F. Flesh

Group 26
Imperious

Find each of the following words on the *Breaking Dawn* page number provided. Based on the way each word is used in the book, guess at its definition.

1. **Rankled** (p. 456) might mean _____

   _____

2. **Ire** (p. 459) might mean _____

   _____

3. **Wary** (p. 460) might mean _____

   _____

4. **Imperiously** (p. 462) might mean _____

   _____

5. **Formidable** (p. 466) might mean _____

   _____

6. **Tenor** (p. 468) might mean _____

   _____

7. **Acquiescence** (p. 471) might mean _____

   _____

8. **Piquing** (p. 475) might mean _____

   _____

Let's see how you did. Check your answers, write the exact definitions, and reread the sentence in *Breaking Dawn* where each word appears. Then complete the drills on the next page.

Definitions

1. **Rankled** (p. 456) means *irritated*. Synonyms: affronted, galled, irked, piqued, vexed.

2. **Ire** (p. 459) means *anger,* and reminds me of the great standardized test word *irate,* which means *angry.* Synonyms: fury, wrath.

3. **Wary** (p. 460) means *worried and watchful* and comes from the word *aware,* which is what you are when you are **worried and watchful.** Synonyms: chary, circumspect, vigilant. *Circumspect* is a great word to break apart. *Circum-* means *around,* as in *circle* and *circumnavigate* (sail **around** something), and *spect-* implies *look,* as in *spectacles* (eyeglasses). So *circumspect* means *looking around—watchful.*

4. **Imperiously** (p. 462) means *bossily;* Renesmee is definitely the **boss!** Here's another *Defining Harry Potter* moment. The **Imperius** Curse, one of the three Unforgivable Curses, gives the caster **control** over another person—pretty **bossy!** Synonym: peremptory.

5. **Formidable** (p. 466) means *very powerful.*

6. **Tenor** (p. 468) means *tone.* Synonym: timbre. *Tenor* can also refer to the *highest male singing voice.*

7. **Acquiescence** (p. 471) means *reluctant acceptance.* Bella has **given in** to Alice's birthday plans, again. In fact, I don't think Bella has ever avoided **acquiescing** to Alice's plans for gifts or a party; Alice is very persuasive, and it's not even her special vampire ability (which is, of course, the ability to foresee the future). Synonyms: assent, compliance, concession, submission.

8. **Piquing** (p. 475) in this case means *stimulating.* That's easy to remember since *piquing* sounds so much like *picking* or even *pricking.* Synonym: whetting. You learned *piqued* above as a synonym for *rankled* (irritated). This is a perfect example of a word with several meanings that the SAT, ACT, GED, or SSAT might use in a reading comprehension question.

Synonyms: Select the word or phrase whose meaning is closest to the word in capital letters.

1. IRE
   A. tenor
   B. wrath
   C. proximity
   D. superciliousness
   E. insouciance

2. WARY
   A. circumspect
   B. formidable
   C. penitent
   D. incendiary
   E. anomalous

3. IMPERIOUS
   A. piquing
   B. whetting
   C. submissive
   D. galling
   E. peremptory

4. ACQUIESCENT
   A. compliant
   B. irate
   C. vexed
   D. petulant
   E. bellicose

Analogies: Select the answer choice that best completes the meaning of the sentence.

5. Dictator is to imperious as
   A. baker is to formidable
   B. president is to propitiated
   C. architect is to clandestine
   D. follower is to acquiescent
   E. musician is to pugnacious

6. Rankled is to irked as
   A. affronted is to eliminated
   B. mitigated is to circumnavigated
   C. piqued is to galled
   D. vexed is to assented
   E. alleviated is to boggled

Sentence Completions: Choose the word that, when inserted in the sentence, <u>best</u> fits the meaning of the sentence as a whole.

7. Larry and Julie _____ the win to Alex; they realized that he had the upper hand and would surely win the game in the end.
   A. acquiesced
   B. piqued
   C. chided
   D. rankled
   E. rebuked

8. The guest speaker at the convention was _____; he kept his presentation neutral for fear of offending the audience.
   A. formidable
   B. omnipresent
   C. inviolate
   D. imperious
   E. circumspect

1. **B.** *Ire* and *wrath* mean *anger*. *Tenor* means *tone*, *proximity* means *nearness*, *superciliousness* means *arrogance*, and *insouciance* means *lack of concern*.

2. **A.** *Wary* and *circumspect* mean *cautious*. *Formidable* means *very powerful*, *penitent* means *regretful*, *incendiary* means *burnable*, and *anomalous* means *abnormal*.

3. **E.** *Imperious* and *peremptory* mean *bossy*. As always, use the process of elimination to find the closest answer—cross off answers that you are **sure** don't work and choose the best of what's left. *Piquing* and *whetting* mean *stimulating*, *submissive* means *reluctantly giving in*, and *galling* means *irritating*.

4. **A.** *Acquiescent* and *compliant* mean *reluctantly accepting*. *Irate* means *angry*, *vexed* means *irritated*, *petulant* means *irritable*, and *bellicose* means *hostile*.

5. **D.** "A dictator is imperious (bossy)."
   - A. A baker is formidable (very powerful) . . . not necessarily.
   - B. A president is propitiated (pleasing, soothing) . . . not necessarily.
   - C. An architect is clandestine (secret) . . . no.
   - (D.) A follower is acquiescent (reluctantly giving in) . . . yes.
   - E. A musician is pugnacious (hostile) . . . no.

   The correct answer should be clearly and directly related, such as defining the first word using the second.

6. **C.** "Rankled (irritated) means irked (irritated)."
   - A. Affronted (irritated) means eliminated . . . no.
   - B. Mitigated (lessened, soothed) means circumnavigated (sailed around) . . . no.
   - (C.) Piqued (irritated) means galled (irritated) . . . yes.
   - D. Vexed (irritated) means assented (reluctantly accepted) . . . no.
   - E. Alleviated (lessened, soothed) means boggled (staggered) . . . no.

7. **A.** "Larry and Julie _surrendered_ the win to Alex; they realized that he had the upper hand and would surely win the game in the end."

   Acquiesced means *reluctantly gave in* and fits best.

8. **E.** "The guest speaker at the convention was _neutral/afraid_; he kept his presentation neutral for fear of offending the audience."

   Circumspect means *cautious* and fits best. Use the process of elimination. *Formidable* means *very powerful*, *omnipresent* means *all-present*, *inviolate* means *undamaged*, and *imperious* means *bossy*.

Superlative Gift

Find each of the following words on the *Breaking Dawn* page number provided. Based on the way each word is used in the book, guess at its definition.

1. **Superlatives** (p. 479) might mean _____

   _____

2. **Eclectic** (p. 479) might mean _____

   _____

3. **Contemporary** (p. 479) might mean _____

   _____

4. **Pristine** (p. 481) might mean _____

   _____

5. **Epitome** (p. 482) might mean _____

   _____

6. **Conundrum** (p. 482) might mean _____

   _____

7. **Diffuse** (p. 487) might mean _____

   _____

8. **Ornately** (p. 487) might mean _____

   _____

Let's see how you did. Check your answers, write the exact definitions, and reread the sentence in *Breaking Dawn* where each word appears. Then complete the drills on the next page.

1. **Superlatives** (p. 479) means *exaggerations,* which makes sense since *super-* means *beyond,* like **beyond** *reality—exaggerated.* Synonym: hyperboles. You learned *hyperbole* (a very exaggerated statement) in Group 16 when you learned that *hyper-* means *very. Superlatives* are usually *exaggerations of* **praise,** like "This is the nicest cottage in the history of cottages!" whereas *hyperboles* are *exaggerations of any kind,* praise or criticism.

2. **Eclectic** (p. 479) means *from varied sources.* This sentence in *Breaking Dawn* reminds me of an SAT sentence completion question; Bella describes *eclectic* right in the sentence, "not one of them matching another." Synonyms: disparate, heterogeneous, manifold, motley, multifarious, sundry, variegated.

3. **Contemporary** (p. 479) means *modern.* Synonym: modish (modern and fashionable).

4. **Pristine** (p. 481) means *pure* or *perfect.* Synonyms: immaculate, intact, virgin.

5. **Epitome** (p. 482) means *perfect* or *highest example of.* Bella means that their honeymoon on the island was the **perfect or highest point** of her human life. Synonyms: paragon, quintessence.

6. **Conundrum** (p. 482) means *riddle* or *a confusing (and sometimes amusing) problem,* such as the one Bella is currently considering! Synonym: quandary.

7. **Diffuse** (p. 487) in this case means *spread out.* It can also mean *wordy,* which is a great chance to bring up one of the SAT's favorite sets of synonyms: *circumlocutory, digressive, discursive, effusive, garrulous, loquacious, periphrastic, prolix, and verbose,* which all mean *chatty* or *wordy.* But, in *Breaking Dawn,* Bella definitely means *spread out* when she describes the sun glinting on Edward's diamond-like body.

8. **Ornately** (p. 487) means *in a fancy way.* Synonym: elaborately, flamboyantly, lavishly, luxuriously, opulently.

Synonyms: Select the word or phrase whose meaning is closest to the word in capital letters.

1. SUPERLATIVE
   A. conundrum
   B. quandary
   C. tenor
   D. adjudication
   E. hyperbole

2. ECLECTIC
   A. ornate
   B. motley
   C. modish
   D. piquing
   E. acquiescent

3. PRISTINE
   A. disparate
   B. heterogeneous
   C. multifarious
   D. immaculate
   E. imperious

4. EPITOME
   A. conundrum
   B. insurgence
   C. paragon
   D. inferno
   E. eventuality

Analogies: Select the answer choice that best completes the meaning of the sentence.

5. Intact is to pristine as
   A. eclectic is to formidable
   B. contemporary is to modish
   C. diffuse is to circumspect
   D. ornate is to irate
   E. petulant is to surreptitious

6. Verbose is to prolix as
   A. discursive is to sanguine
   B. digressive is to aberrant
   C. periphrastic is to viscous
   D. loquacious is to effusive
   E. garrulous is to ardent

Sentence Completions: Choose the word that, when inserted in the sentence, <u>best</u> fits the meaning of the sentence as a whole.

7. Chloe was proud of her collection of Beatles' records; they were _____, hardly ever used and still in their original jackets.
   A. diffuse
   B. ornate
   C. pristine
   D. contemporary
   E. heterogeneous

8. The advisor of the school paper warned students against using _____ expressions that exaggerate what they intend to convey.
   A. eclectic
   B. superlative
   C. prosaic
   D. pensive
   E. spurious

114

Solutions

1. **E.** *Superlative* and *hyperbole* mean *exaggeration. Conundrum* and *quandary* mean *confusing problem, tenor* means *tone,* and *adjudication* means *judgment.*

2. **B.** *Eclectic* means *from varied sources,* so *motley* (varied) is the best choice. *Ornate* means *fancy, modish* means *modern and fashionable, piquing* means *stimulating,* and *acquiescent* means *reluctantly accepting.*

3. **D.** *Pristine* and *immaculate* mean *pure. Disparate, heterogeneous,* and *multifarious* mean *varied. Imperious* means *bossy.*

4. **C.** *Epitome* and *paragon* mean *highest example of. Conundrum* means *confusing problem, insurgence* means *rebellion, inferno* means *huge fire,* and *eventuality* means *possibility.*

5. **B.** "Intact (undamaged) means pristine (pure)."
   A. Eclectic (varied) means formidable (powerful) . . . no.
   (B.) Contemporary (modern) means modish (modern and fashionable) . . . yes.
   C. Diffuse (spread out) means circumspect (cautious) . . . no.
   D. Ornate (fancy) means irate (angry) . . . no.
   E. Petulant (irritable) means surreptitious (secret) . . . no.

6. **D.** "Verbose (wordy) means prolix (wordy)."
   A. Discursive (wordy) means sanguine (optimistic) . . . no.
   B. Digressive (wordy) means aberrant (abnormal) . . . no.
   C. Periphrastic (wordy) means viscous (thick and gooey) . . . no.
   (D.) Loquacious (wordy) means effusive (wordy) . . . yes.
   E. Garrulous (wordy) means ardent (passionate) . . . no.

7. **C.** "Chloe was proud of her collection of Beatles' records; they were _hardly used_, hardly ever used and still in their original jackets."
   Pristine means *perfect* or *pure* and fits best.

8. **B.** "The advisor of the school paper warned students against using _exaggerated_ expressions that exaggerate what they intend to convey."
   Superlative means *exaggerated* and fits best. The advisor may have warned students against expressions that are *eclectic* (from varied sources), *prosaic* (ordinary and unimaginative), *pensive* (thoughtful), or *spurious* (doubtful), but you have evidence **only** that the advisor warned against "expressions that exaggerate what they intend to convey," so choice B fits best. Base your answer on the info directly stated in the sentence.

Group 28

Gravity

Find each of the following words on the *Breaking Dawn* page number provided. Based on the way each word is used in the book, guess at its definition.

1. **Monstrosity** (p. 487) might mean _____

_____

2. **Expletive** (p. 488) might mean _____

_____

3. **Talisman** (p. 493) might mean _____

_____

4. **Ward** (p. 498) might mean _____

_____

5. **Concave** (p. 501) might mean _____

_____

6. **Solemn** (p. 503) might mean _____

_____

7. **Grave** (p. 503) might mean _____

_____

8. **Levity** (p. 505) might mean _____

_____

Let's see how you did. Check your answers, write the exact definitions, and reread the sentence in *Breaking Dawn* where each word appears. Then complete the drills on the next page.

Definitions

1. **Monstrosity** (p. 487) comes from *monster* and means *something large, outrageous, and unattractive.* Alice has style, so the closet of clothes she set up for Bella is definitely not **unattractive,** but it certainly is **outrageously large!**

2. **Expletive** (p. 488) means *swear word.* Synonyms: blasphemy, cuss, imprecation, obscenity, profanity. You learned that *blasphemy* from Group 22 means *disrespect for sacred things.* You can see the connection.

3. **Talisman** (p. 493) means *magical lucky charm,* like the crystal skull that Indiana Jones was hunting down in *Indiana Jones and the Kingdom of the Crystal Skull.* Synonyms: amulet, fetish, juju, totem.

4. **Ward** (p. 498) can mean *dependent,* which is how Jacob is using it on page 498, but it can also mean *department, district,* or *lookout.*

5. **Concave** (p. 501) means *curved inward* and even sounds like *caved.* In fact, *con-* means *with,* so *concaved* means *with cave—curved inward.* You probably learned this word in geometry class when you studied polygons or in physics class when you studied lenses. The opposite of *concave* is *convex* (curved out). Synonym: recessed.

6. **Solemn** (p. 503) means *serious.* Synonyms: earnest, grave, sober, somber.

7. **Grave** (p. 503) is a synonym for *solemn* and also means *serious.* It is related to the word *gravity,* which can mean *serious or heavy*—the same word for the force that keeps your feet on the ground. I love this scene in the book: Edward is very **serious,** warning Renesmee not to bite Charlie, but she asks if it's okay to bite Jacob. She's the best!

8. **Levity** (p. 505) means *humor* or *lightness* (as opposed to *seriousness*). Synonyms: frivolity, gaiety, glee, jocularity, jollity, joviality, lightheartedness, merriment, mirth. The opposite of *levity* is *gravity* (seriousness) or the fancy related word *gravitas* (seriousness of demeanor). Why do you think high school singing groups are called **glee** clubs? Turns out it's not because they usually look so **lighthearted and jolly** when they sing, or even because the Fox TV show *Glee* is so darn **humorous,** but because original **glee** clubs in the 1600s sang short songs that were called **glees.**

Synonyms: Select the word or phrase whose meaning is closest to the word in capital letters.

1. EXPLETIVE
   A. imprecation
   B. monstrosity
   C. amulet
   D. fetish
   E. totem

2. TALISMAN
   A. conundrum
   B. revelation
   C. ward
   D. totem
   E. horde

3. SOLEMN
   A. concave
   B. convex
   C. verbose
   D. effusive
   E. grave

4. LEVITY
   A. gravitas
   B. glee
   C. petulance
   D. acquiescence
   E. ire

Analogies: Select the answer choice that best completes the meaning of the sentence.

5. Gravitas is to frivolity as
   A. reproach is to censure
   B. insouciance is to indifference
   C. antipathy is to amiability
   D. negligence is to carelessness
   E. trepidation is to foreboding

6. Sphere is to convex as
   A. bitten apple is to concave
   B. talisman is to ward
   C. half orange is to expletive
   D. vampire is to diamond
   E. bowl is to nebulously

Sentence Completions: Choose the word that, when inserted in the sentence, <u>best</u> fits the meaning of the sentence as a whole.

7. Normally jocular and frivolous, her mood changed to _____ as she entered the haunted crypt.
   A. lightheartedness
   B. merriment
   C. feebleness
   D. jubilance
   E. somberness

8. When Eudora heard the disappointing news, she let slip a few _____ that she immediately regretted because she was on national television.
   A. loams
   B. smiles
   C. edicts
   D. mandates
   E. imprecations

1. **A.** *Expletive* and *imprecation* mean *curse word. Monstrosity* means *something large, outrageous,* and *unattractive. Amulet, fetish,* and *totem* mean *magical lucky charm.*

2. **D.** *Talisman* and *totem* mean *magical lucky charm. Conundrum* means *confusing problem, revelation* means *realization, ward* means *dependent,* and *horde* means *mob.*

3. **E.** *Solemn* and *grave* mean *serious. Concave* means *curved in, convex* means *curved out,* and *verbose* and *effusive* mean *wordy.*

4. **B.** *Levity* and *glee* mean *lightness. Gravitas* means *serious demeanor, petulance* means *irritability, acquiescence* means *reluctant acceptance,* and *ire* means *anger.*

5. **C.** "Gravitas (serious demeanor) is the opposite of frivolity (light demeanor)."

    A. Reproach (scolding) is the opposite of censure (scolding) . . . no.

    B. Insouciance (casualness) is the opposite of indifference (casualness) . . . no.

    (C.) Antipathy (dislike) is the opposite of amiability (friendliness) . . . yes.

    D. Negligence (lack of care) is the opposite of carelessness . . . no.

    E. Trepidation (fear) is the opposite of foreboding (fear) . . . no.

    Using the process of elimination, choice C is best.

6. **A.** "A sphere is convex (curved out) shaped."

    (A.) A bitten apple is concave (curved in) shaped . . . maybe.

    B. A talisman is ward (dependent) shaped . . . no.

    C. A half orange is expletive (curse) shaped . . . no.

    D. A vampire is diamond shaped . . . no.

    E. A bowl is nebulously (unclearly) shaped . . . no.

    Choice A is the best answer.

7. **E.** "Normally jocular and frivolous, her mood changed to <u>not jocular</u> as she entered the haunted crypt."

    Jocular means *lighthearted and joking.* However, since you want the opposite of *jocular, somberness* (seriousness) is the best answer.

8. **E.** "When Eudora heard the disappointing news, she let slip a few <u>disappointed expressions</u> that she immediately regretted because she was on national television."

    Imprecations means *curse words* and best fits the evidence "disappointing news."

Group 29

Euphoria

Find each of the following words on the *Breaking Dawn* page number provided. Based on the way each word is used in the book, guess at its definition.

1. **Abashed** (p. 505) might mean _____

   _____

2. **Innuendos** (p. 511) might mean _____

   _____

3. **Complementary** (p. 525) might mean _____

   _____

4. **Cordial** (p. 526) might mean _____

   _____

5. **Euphoric** (p. 527) might mean _____

   _____

6. **Soprano** (p. 528) might mean _____

   _____

7. **Verifiable** (p. 528) might mean _____

   _____

8. **Hybrids** (p. 542) might mean _____

   _____

Let's see how you did. Check your answers, write the exact definitions, and reread the sentence in *Breaking Dawn* where each word appears. Then complete the drills on the next page.

Definitions

1. **Abashed** (p. 505) means *embarrassed*. Carlisle was **embarrassed** to be caught lying—he had been telling Charlie that Bella was in Atlanta at the Centers for Disease Control and Prevention. I bet it's not too often that Carlisle gets caught lying, or even lies in the first place.

2. **Innuendos** (p. 511) means *suggestive hints*. Emmett's suggestive hints are annoying me. Don't get me wrong, I love his levity and his jocular approach to life, but Bella needs his support during Charlie's visit. Synonym: insinuations.

3. **Complementary** (p. 525) means *combining to improve each other*. Synonyms: compatible, harmonious, reciprocal. Another related word is *interdependent,* which means *dependent on each other.*

4. **Cordial** (p. 526) means *friendly*. Synonyms: affable, amiable, convivial, genial.

5. **Euphoric** (p. 527) means *thrilled* and was a synonym for *exultant* in Group 21. Synonyms: buoyant, ebullient, ecstatic, elated, exultant, jubilant, rapturous.

6. **Soprano** (p. 528) means *the highest singing voice*. It makes sense that Renesmee would have a **high voice**—at only seven days old, she is the youngest baby in history to speak!

7. **Verifiable** (p. 528) means *confirmable,* as in to **confirm** the truth of something. Everything Carlisle and Edward found in their research was *circumstantial* (indirect) and they could not **confirm** the truth of it. The word part *veri-* refers to *truth,* which helps you remember words like *verity* (a fundamental **truth**), *veracity* (**truthfulness**), and *verisimilitude* (the appearance of seeming **true**). *Verisimilitude* is a great standardized test word that you don't hear too often, except from Jim in *American Pie* when he's at Stifler's party at the beginning of the movie demonstrating his excellent vocabulary and wondering why, even still, he can't speak confidently to girls. *Verisimilitude* might not help you at parties, but it's a terrific SAT word that's sure to earn you standardized-test points!

8. **Hybrids** (p. 542) means *mixtures*. Synonyms: amalgamations, fusions.

Synonyms: Select the word or phrase whose meaning is closest to the word in capital letters.

1. ABASHED
   A. affable
   B. amiable
   C. convivial
   D. embarrassed
   E. complementary

2. CORDIAL
   A. genial
   B. complementary
   C. soprano
   D. lugubrious
   E. grave

3. EUPHORIC
   A. eclectic
   B. ebullient
   C. somber
   D. intact
   E. immaculate

4. VERIFIABLE
   A. interdependent
   B. heterogeneous
   C. motley
   D. multifarious
   E. confirmable

Analogies: Select the answer choice that best completes the meaning of the sentence.

5. Hybrid is to amalgamation as
   A. verisimilitude is to believability
   B. verity is to elation
   C. levity is to gravitas
   D. ornate is to pristine
   E. superlative is to motley

6. Euphoric is to lugubrious as
   A. ecstatic is to buoyant
   B. exultant is to elated
   C. jubilant is to affable
   D. rapturous is to amiable
   E. ebullient is to doleful

Sentence Completions: Choose the word that, when inserted in the sentence, <u>best</u> fits the meaning of the sentence as a whole.

7. Frank hoped that using the real names of towns would give his fictitious short story some _____.
   A. euphoria
   B. innuendos
   C. levity
   D. verisimilitude
   E. propinquity

8. Mina was abashed when she realized that her teacher viewed her _____ not as amiable but as sycophantic.
   A. insinuations
   B. petulance
   C. imperiousness
   D. rhetoric
   E. affability

1. **D.** *Abashed* means *embarrassed*. *Affable, amiable,* and *convivial* mean *friendly*. *Complementary* means *combining to improve each other.*

2. **A.** *Cordial* and *genial* mean *friendly*. *Complementary* means *combining to improve each other, soprano* means *highest singing voice, lugubrious* means *gloomy,* and *grave* means *serious.*

3. **B.** *Euphoric* and *ebullient* mean *thrilled*. *Eclectic* means *from varied sources, somber* means *serious,* and *intact* and *immaculate* mean *undamaged.*

4. **E.** *Verifiable* means *confirmable.* Use the process of elimination. *Interdependent* means *dependent on each other;* and *heterogeneous, motley,* and *multifarious* mean *varied.*

5. **A.** "Hybrid (mixture) means amalgamation (mixture)."
   - (A.) Verisimilitude means believability . . . yes.
   - B. Verity (truth) means elation (thrill) . . . no.
   - C. Levity (lightness) means gravitas (seriousness) . . . no, they are opposites.
   - D. Ornate (fancy) means pristine (pure) . . . no.
   - E. Superlative (exaggeration) means motley (varied) . . . no.

6. **E.** "Euphoric (thrilled) is the opposite of lugubrious (gloomy)."
   - A. Ecstatic (thrilled) is the opposite of buoyant (thrilled) . . . no.
   - B. Exultant (thrilled) is the opposite of elated (thrilled) . . . no.
   - C. Jubilant (thrilled) is the opposite of affable (friendly) . . . no.
   - D. Rapturous (thrilled) is the opposite of amiable (friendly) . . . no.
   - (E.) Ebullient (thrilled) is the opposite of doleful (gloomy) . . . yes.

7. **D.** "Frank hoped that using the real names of towns would give his fictitious short story some <u>realness</u>."

   Choose the answer that is most clearly supported by the evidence in the passage. *Verisimilitude* means *appearance of being real,* and best fits the evidence "using real names of towns." *Euphoria* means *thrill, innuendos* means *suggestive hints, levity* means *lightness,* and *propinquity* means *nearness. Fictitious* means *not true,* but you could get this question correct even if you didn't know that word; if there is a word in the sentence that you don't know, try answering without it.

8. **E.** "Mina was abashed when she realized that her teacher viewed her <u>amiability</u> not as amiable but as sycophantic."

   Affability and *amiability* mean *friendliness. Insinuations* means *suggestive hints, petulance* means *irritability, imperiousness* means *bossiness,* and *rhetoric* means *style.* You may not have known *sycophantic* (flattery used to get something from someone of power), but this is another reminder that you can often get a question correct even if you don't know one of the words in the sentence.

Group 30
Censure

Find each of the following words on the *Breaking Dawn* page number provided. Based on the way each word is used in the book, guess at its definition.

1. **Bane** (p. 547) might mean _____

   _____

2. **Opaque** (p. 551) might mean _____

   _____

3. **Tersely** (p. 557) might mean _____

   _____

4. **Censure** (p. 559) might mean _____

   _____

5. **Circuitous** (p. 563) might mean _____

   _____

6. **Bolstered** (p. 567) might mean _____

   _____

7. **Incognito** (p. 568) might mean _____

   _____

8. **Anesthetize** (p. 575) might mean _____

   _____

Let's see how you did. Check your answers, write the exact definitions, and reread the sentence in *Breaking Dawn* where each word appears. Then complete the drills on the next page.

1. **Bane** (p. 547) means *plague* or *curse*. Bella says that the "immortal children" were "the unmentionable **bane**" as well as the "the appalling taboo." *Taboo* means *something forbidden*. Remember from earlier in *Breaking Dawn* that the "immortal children" were a **plague** to the vampire world, causing great chaos and fighting, so they became **forbidden.**

2. **Opaque** (p. 551) means *solid* or *unclear* or *not transparent* (see-through)—basically something that you can't see through. Figuratively, it can also mean *a difficult or unclear concept that is hard to grasp*. Objects can be *solid* or *not transparent,* and concepts can be *hard to grasp*.

3. **Tersely** (p. 557) means *briefly*. Synonyms (which imply *briefly,* but also *rudely*): brusquely, curtly, laconically.

4. **Censure** (p. 559) means *severe criticism. Censure* was a synonym for *reproach* in Group 4 and *condemn* in Group 16. The other synonyms are *admonishment, castigation, excoriation, obloquy, rebuke, reprimand, reproof,* and *vituperation*. You can use the related word *censor* (edit inappropriate parts from a work of art) to help you remember the meaning of *censure*. You can see how they are related; a person might **censor** (edit) parts that deserve **censure** (criticism).

5. **Circuitous** (p. 563) means *round about*. That's easy to remember, since *circuitous* sounds like *circle*.

6. **Bolstered** (p. 567) means *strengthened*. Standardized tests love to test the opposite word *undermined,* which means *weakened*.

7. **Incognito** (p. 568) means *undercover*.

8. **Anesthetize** (p. 575) means *make unaware*. Synonym: sedate.

Synonyms: Select the word or phrase whose meaning is closest to the word in capital letters.

1. BANE
   A. hybrid
   B. amalgamation
   C. fusion
   D. plague
   E. veracity

2. OPAQUE
   A. circuitous
   B. solid
   C. transparent
   D. cordial
   E. cavalier

3. TERSE
   A. laconic
   B. verbose
   C. prolix
   D. histrionic
   E. contumelious

4. CENSURE
   A. acquiescence
   B. rhetoric
   C. insurrection
   D. lethargy
   E. obloquy

Analogies: Select the answer choice that best completes the meaning of the sentence.

5. Bolster is to undermine as
   A. anesthetize is to rebuke
   B. diffuse is to whet
   C. rankle is to irk
   D. gall is to placate
   E. articulate is to mitigate

6. Double agent is to incognito as
   A. vampire is to curt
   B. werewolf is to laconic
   C. human is to imperious
   D. hybrid is to mixed
   E. dancer is to soprano

Sentence Completions: Choose the word or words that, when inserted in the sentence, best fits the meaning of the sentence as a whole.

7. Ruefully, Hayley considered the bitter _____ that she had received from the town council and realized that it was her own fault that she had become the _____ of the town.
   A. anesthetizing . . amalgamation
   B. bolstering . . fusion
   C. undermining . . horde
   D. censure . . toast
   E. obloquy . . bane

8. Friends consider Sebastian to be _____; he says very little, but what he does say means a lot.
   A. terse
   B. circuitous
   C. opaque
   D. verifiable
   E. loquacious

Solutions

1. **D.** *Bane* means *plague. Hybrid, amalgamation,* and *fusion* mean *mixture;* and *veracity* means *truthfulness.*

2. **B.** *Opaque* means *solid. Circuitous* means *round about, transparent* means *see-through, cordial* means *friendly,* and *cavalier* means *overly casual.*

3. **A.** *Terse* and *laconic* mean *brief. Verbose* and *prolix* mean *wordy, histrionic* means *very dramatic,* and *contumelious* means *harsh and critical.*

4. **E.** *Censure* and *obloquy* mean *harsh criticism.* Use the process of elimination. *Acquiescence* means *reluctant acceptance, rhetoric* means *style, insurrection* means *rebellion,* and *lethargy* means *sluggishness. Lethargy* is related to *lethargic,* which was a synonym for *stagnant* (still or stale) in Group 19.

5. **D.** "Bolster (strengthen) is the opposite of undermine (weaken)."
   A. Anesthetize (make unaware) is the opposite of rebuke (scold) . . . no.
   B. Diffuse (spread out) is the opposite of whet (stimulate) . . . no.
   C. Rankle (irritate) is the opposite of irk (irritate) . . . no.
   D. Gall (irritate) is the opposite of placate (soothe) . . . yes.
   E. Articulate (express clearly) is the opposite of mitigate (lessen) . . . no.

6. **D.** "A double agent is incognito (undercover)."
   A. A vampire is curt (brief) . . . no, not necessarily.
   B. A werewolf is laconic (brief) . . . no, not necessarily.
   C. A human is imperious (bossy) . . . no, not necessarily.
   D. A hybrid is mixed . . . yes, a *hybrid* is by definition *mixed,* just as a double agent is by definition undercover.
   E. A dancer is soprano (highest singing voice) . . . no, not necessarily.

   I'm sure you can think of vampires and werewolves that are laconic, or humans that are bossy, but the words in the correct answer should have a clear and definitive relationship.

7. **E.** "Ruefully, Hayley considered the bitter _bitterness_ that she had received from the town council and realized that it was her own fault that she had become the _????_ of the town."

   Use the process of elimination, one blank at a time. *Obloquy* means *harsh criticism,* and *bane* means *plague,* so choice E works best. Be cautious of choices like *toast* in choice D, which make recognizable phrases ("toast of the town"), but do not fit the evidence in the sentence that you need a negative, rather than a positive, word.

8. **A.** "Friends consider Sebastian to be _saying very little;_ he says very little, but what he does say means a lot."
   Terse means *brief.*

Quiz 6

I. Let's review some of the words that you've seen in Groups 26–30. Match each of the following words to the correct definition or synonym on the right. Then check the solutions on page 172.

1. Wary		A.	Bossy
2. Imperious		B.	Hyperbole
3. Acquiescence		C.	Imprecation
4. Superlative		D.	Circumspect
5. Eclectic		E.	Amulet
6. Pristine		F.	Compliance
7. Expletive		G.	Laconic
8. Talisman		H.	Multifarious
9. Levity		I.	Intact
10. Abashed		J.	Plague
11. Cordial		K.	Confirmable
12. Verifiable		L.	Frivolity
13. Bane		M.	Reproach
14. Terse		N.	Amiable
15. Censure		O.	Embarrassed

II. Let's review several of the word parts that you've seen in Groups 26–30. Match each of the following word parts to the correct definition or synonym on the right. Then check the solutions on page 172.

16. Circum-		A.	Beyond
17. Spect-		B.	Truth
18. Super-		C.	With
19. Hyper-		D.	Around
20. Con-		E.	Very
21. Veri-		F.	Look

Latent Abilities

Find each of the following words on the *Breaking Dawn* page number provided. Based on the way each word is used in the book, guess at its definition.

1. **Latent** (p. 580) might mean _____

   _____

2. **Nebulous** (p. 580) might mean _____

   _____

3. **Heinous** (p. 580) might mean _____

   _____

4. **Finesse** (p. 584) might mean _____

   _____

5. **Trysts** (p. 587) might mean _____

   _____

6. **Unprecedented** (p. 592) might mean _____

   _____

7. **Subjective** (p. 596) might mean _____

   _____

8. **Haphazard** (p. 596) might mean _____

   _____

Let's see how you did. Check your answers, write the exact definitions,
and reread the sentence in *Breaking Dawn* where each word appears.
Then complete the drills on the next page.

1. **Latent** (p. 580) means *hidden* or *temporarily inactive*. Synonyms:
   abeyant, dormant, quiescent.

2. **Nebulous** (p. 580) means *unclear*. Synonyms: ambiguous,
   amorphous, equivocal, imprecise, muddled, tenuous, vague.
   Amorphous is an interesting word to break apart. *A-* means *not*
   or *without,* and *morph-* means *form* or *shape,* so *amorphous* means
   without shape—unclear.

3. **Heinous** (p. 580) means *wicked* or *worthy of hatred*. Synonyms:
   abhorrent, abominable, baleful, depraved, egregious, execrable,
   impious, iniquitous, malevolent, nefarious, odious, pernicious,
   reprehensible, villainous. Those are a lot of words that mean
   worthy of hatred. What do you think; does Alice's behavior seem
   abhorrent as well as all of these other fifteen synonyms of *worthy
   of hatred,* or does she have a plan?

4. **Finesse** (p. 584) means *skill and grace*. Synonyms: flair, poise.

5. **Trysts** (p. 587) means *romantic encounters*. Technically, a tryst is
   a ***private*** *romantic encounter,* but I think the word *private* is a bit
   redundant in the definition; what sort of romantic encounter
   (outside of high school, of course) is not private?

6. **Unprecedented** (p. 592) means *unheard of before*. A *precedent* is *an
   earlier example,* as in Claude Debussy's famous quote, "As there
   are no precedents, I must create anew." Claude Debussy is best
   known as a central figure in French Impressionist music and, of
   course, as Bella and Edward's favorite composer!

7. **Subjective** (p. 596) means *intuitive* or *based on one's own ideas*. The
   opposite of *subjective* is *objective* (factual).

8. **Haphazard** (p. 596) means *unpredictable*.

Synonyms: Select the word or phrase whose meaning is closest to the word in capital letters.

1. LATENT
   A. ambiguous
   B. amorphous
   C. equivocal
   D. abeyant
   E. objective

2. NEBULOUS
   A. haphazard
   B. baleful
   C. terse
   D. circuitous
   E. imprecise

3. HEINOUS
   A. ephemeral
   B. evanescent
   C. transient
   D. odious
   E. genteel

4. SUBJECTIVE
   A. urbane
   B. personal
   C. objective
   D. surreptitious
   E. supercilious

Analogies: Select the answer choice that best completes the meaning of the sentence.

5. Subjective is to objective as
   A. haphazard is to omniscient
   B. unprecedented is to pernicious
   C. execrable is to baleful
   D. iniquitous is to nefarious
   E. veneration is to enmity

6. Heinous is to pernicious as
   A. abhorrent is to abominable
   B. reprehensible is to nebulous
   C. baleful is to muddled
   D. depraved is to equivocal
   E. impious is to quiescent

Sentence Completions: Choose the word that, when inserted in the sentence, best fits the meaning of the sentence as a whole.

7. Luis was famous for his style and _____; he could handle any situation with grace.
   A. dissension
   B. chagrin
   C. animosity
   D. evanescence
   E. finesse

8. As time went on, Harry realized that his feelings for Ginny had always been there, but were previously _____.
   A. latent
   B. trysts
   C. objective
   D. sanguine
   E. ephemeral

1. **D.** *Latent* and *abeyant* mean *temporarily inactive. Ambiguous, amorphous,* and *equivocal* mean *unclear;* and *objective* means *factual.*

2. **E.** *Nebulous* and *imprecise* mean *unclear. Haphazard* means *unpredictable, baleful* means *wicked, terse* means *brief,* and *circuitous* means *round about.*

3. **D.** *Heinous* and *odious* mean *wicked* or *worthy of hatred. Ephemeral, evanescent,* and *transient* mean *temporary,* and *genteel* means *stylish and charming.*

4. **B.** *Subjective* means *based on one's own ideas (personal). Urbane* means *stylish and charming, objective* means *factual, surreptitious* means *secret,* and *supercilious* means *arrogant.*

5. **E.** "Subjective (based on one's own ideas) is the opposite of objective (factual)."

   A . Haphazard (unpredictable) is the opposite of omniscient (all-knowing) . . . no.

   B . Unprecedented (new) is the opposite of pernicious (wicked) . . . no.

   C . Execrable (worthy of hatred) is the opposite of baleful (wicked) . . . no.

   D. Iniquitous (wicked) is the opposite of nefarious (wicked) . . . no.

   (E.) Veneration (respect) is the opposite of enmity (hostility) . . . yes.

6. **A.** "Heinous (wicked) means pernicious (wicked)."

   (A.) Abhorrent (worthy of hatred) means abominable (worthy of hatred) . . . yes.

   B . Reprehensible (wicked) means nebulous (unclear) . . . no.

   C . Baleful (wicked) means muddled (unclear) . . . no.

   D. Depraved (wicked) means equivocal (unclear) . . . no.

   E . Impious (wicked) means quiescent (temporarily inactive) . . . no.

7. **E.** "Luis was famous for his style and <u>grace</u>; he could handle any situation with grace."

   Finesse means *skill and grace* and fits best.

8. **A.** "As time went on, Harry realized that his feelings for Ginny had always been there, but were previously <u>????</u>."

   If you can't think of a word to fill the blank, use the process of elimination. *Latent* means *hidden* or *temporarily inactive* and best fits the evidence "had always been there." You have no evidence that Harry's feelings were previously *objective* (factual), *sanguine* (optimistic and cheerful), or *ephemeral* (temporary). Choice B, *trysts,* is an appealing answer since it means *romantic encounters,* which relates to the sentence, but it does **not** fit into the blank. That's why you think of a word for the blank before you look at the choices, to avoid this trap.

Group 32

Thwarted Attacks?

Find each of the following words on the *Breaking Dawn* page number provided. Based on the way each word is used in the book, guess at its definition.

1. **Macabre** (p. 597) might mean _____

   _____

2. **Thwarted** (p. 598) might mean _____

   _____

3. **Radius** (p. 599) might mean _____

   _____

4. **Castigating** (p. 601) might mean _____

   _____

5. **Repentant** (p. 602) might mean _____

   _____

6. **Sardonically** (p. 604) might mean _____

   _____

7. **Pretext** (p. 605) might mean _____

   _____

8. **Pretense** (p. 605) might mean _____

   _____

Let's see how you did. Check your answers, write the exact definitions, and reread the sentence in *Breaking Dawn* where each word appears. Then complete the drills on the next page.

1. **Macabre** (p. 597) means *gruesome*. Synonyms: ghastly, gory, grisly, grotesque, hideous, morbid. Can you remember the scene from *New Moon* that Bella is referring to? What was **gruesome** about it? Hint: Remember the forty tourists that Heidi led into the room.

2. **Thwarted** (p. 598) means *prevented* or *blocked*. Synonyms: foiled, forestalled, stonewalled, stymied.

3. **Radius** (p. 599) refers to *the thicker of the two forearm bones*. The other, thinner bone, is called the *ulna*. *Radius,* as Bella's math teacher, Mr. Varner, could tell you, also refers to *the length from a circle to the center of the circle*.

4. **Castigating** (p. 601) means *severely scolding*. *Castigation* was a synonym for *censure* in Group 30. Synonyms for *castigate:* admonish, censure, chastise, chide, condemn, excoriate, rebuke, reprehend, reprimand, reproach, reproof, vituperate.

5. **Repentant** (p. 602) means *regretful for wrongdoing*. Synonyms: contrite, penitent, remorseful.

6. **Sardonically** (p. 604) means *sarcastically (disrespectfully mocking)*. In the cable television show *Monk,* Monk's brilliant brother, Ambrose, defines *sardonic,* "You were being **sardonic**. Sarcasm is a contemptuous ironic statement. You were being mockingly derisive. That's **sardonic**." ("Mr. Monk and the Three Pigs," USA Cable Network, 2002). He means that *sardonic* is a bit meaner than *sarcastic*. Technically he's right, but the SAT, ACT, GED, SSAT, and most people use them as synonyms. Monk and his brother do tend to be a *bit* particular about things.

7. **Pretext** (p. 605) means *false reason justifying an action*. Synonyms: facade, guise (like a superhero's disguise), pretense, ruse.

8. **Pretense** (p. 605) means *false display*. Synonyms: facade, guise, pretext, ruse. The Volturi used Irina's report of an "Immortal Child" as a *pretext* (false reason) for their *pretense* (false display) of punishment, when in fact they want to add the gifted Cullens into their guard.

Synonyms: Select the word or phrase whose meaning is closest to the word in capital letters.

1. MACABRE
   A. remorseful
   B. penitent
   C. contrite
   D. morbid
   E. capacious

2. THWART
   A. goad
   B. foment
   C. prod
   D. spur
   E. stymie

3. CASTIGATE
   A. excoriate
   B. bolster
   C. undermine
   D. acquiesce
   E. indemnify

4. REPENTANT
   A. sardonic
   B. contrite
   C. sarcastic
   D. grisly
   E. foiled

Analogies: Select the answer choice that best completes the meaning of the sentence.

5. Pretext is to pretense as
   A. facade is to sarcasm
   B. guise is to ruse
   C. radius is to verity
   D. tryst is to antipathy
   E. verisimilitude is to morose

6. Repentant is to contrite as
   A. fleeting is to cavalier
   B. apathetic is to insouciant
   C. clandestine is to voluminous
   D. covert is to consummate
   E. surreptitious is to pedestrian

Sentence Completions: Choose the word or words that, when inserted in the sentence, <u>best</u> fits the meaning of the sentence as a whole.

7. Many critics feel that Cavallo's films are not so grotesque as to be called _____.
   A. brusque
   B. terse
   C. treacly
   D. macabre
   E. sardonic

8. Though the judge harshly _____ Lang for the crime, he was moved by Lang's expression of _____ and promised a reduced fine.
   A. castigated .. pretense
   B. presaged .. contrition
   C. rebuked .. remorse
   D. desiccated .. penitence
   E. reproached .. finesse

1. **D.** *Macabre* and *morbid* mean *gruesome. Remorseful, penitent,* and *contrite* mean *regretful;* and *capacious* means *very roomy.*

2. **E.** *Thwart* and *stymie* mean *block. Goad, foment, prod,* and *spur* mean *provoke.*

3. **A.** *Castigate* and *excoriate* mean *scold severely. Bolster* means *strengthen, undermine* means *weaken, acquiesce* means *reluctantly accept,* and *indemnify* means *pay back for.*

4. **B.** *Repentant* and *contrite* mean *regretful.* Use the process of elimination—cross off answers that you are **sure** don't work and choose the best of what's left. *Sardonic* and *sarcastic* mean *disrespectfully mocking, grisly* means *gruesome,* and *foiled* means *blocked.*

5. **B.** "Pretext (false reason) is similar to pretense (false display)."
   A. Facade (false display) is similar to sarcasm (disrespectful mocking) . . . no.
   (B.) Guise (false display) is similar to ruse (false display) . . . yes.
   C. Radius (arm bone) is similar to verity (truth) . . . no.
   D. Tryst (romantic encounter) is similar to antipathy (hostility) . . . no.
   E. Verisimilitude (believability) is similar to morose (gloomy) . . . no.

   If you need to use a complex explanation and tell a long story to make an answer choice work, then it is not the correct choice. The words in the correct answer should be clearly and directly related.

6. **B.** "Repentant means contrite (regretful)."
   A. Fleeting (temporary) means cavalier (overly casual) . . . no.
   (B.) Apathetic (not caring) means insouciant (not caring) . . . yes.
   C. Clandestine (secret) means voluminous (very spacious) . . . no.
   D. Covert (secret) means consummate (absolute) . . . no.
   E. Surreptitious (secret) means pedestrian (ordinary and unimaginative) . . . no.

7. **D.** "Many critics feel that Cavallo's films are not so grotesque as to be called *grotesque*."
   Macabre and *grotesque* mean *gruesome.*

8. **C.** "Though the judge harshly *harshed* Lang for the crime, he was moved by Lang's expression of *????* and promised a reduced fine."
   Use the process of elimination. *Rebuked* means *criticized severely*, and *remorse* means *regret*.

Burgundy Eyes

Find each of the following words on the *Breaking Dawn* page number provided. Based on the way each word is used in the book, guess at its definition.

1. **Rangy** (p. 610) might mean _____

   _____

2. **Misanthropic** (p. 611) might mean _____

   _____

3. **Obscure** (p. 613) might mean _____

   _____

4. **Goad** (p. 621) might mean _____

   _____

5. **Pacify** (p. 621) might mean _____

   _____

6. **Egregiously** (p. 626) might mean _____

   _____

7. **In tandem** (p. 626) might mean _____

   _____

8. **Burgundy** (p. 627) might mean _____

   _____

Let's see how you did. Check your answers, write the exact definitions,
and reread the sentence in *Breaking Dawn* where each word appears.
Then complete the drills on the next page.

1. **Rangy** (p. 610) means *long and slender.*

2. **Misanthropic** (p. 611) means *antisocial.* You get lots of hints to the
   meaning of *misanthropic* in *Breaking Dawn;* Alistair "could hardly
   stand a visit," "preferred to wander alone," and "shunned all
   company." In fact, *mis-* comes from *misein,* which means *hate,* and
   anthrop- refers to *people* (or vampires in this case), so *misanthropic*
   means *hating people.* The opposite of *misanthropic* is *gregarious*
   (outgoing and friendly).

3. **Obscure** (p. 613) means *unclear* or *difficult to understand.* It is
   difficult to understand why Alice disappeared, but I trust her.
   Two high-level synonyms for *obscure* are *abstruse* and *recondite.*
   You've now joined the club of fourteen people on the planet who
   know these words, but that's good because I've seen these words
   many times on the SAT.

4. **Goad** (p. 621) means *provoke* or *urge,* like when Homer says,
   "Nobody calls me chicken without **goading** me into doing
   something stupid!" (*The Simpsons,* "Love, Springfieldian Style,"
   FOX, 2008). Synonyms: incite, prod, spur.

5. **Pacify** (p. 621) sounds a bit like *peace* and means *make peaceful* or
   soothe. Synonyms: allay, ameliorate, appease, assuage, conciliate,
   mollify, palliate, placate, propitiate.

6. **Egregiously** (p. 626) means *very badly.*

7. **In tandem** (p. 626) means *together,* "their voices so similar that less
   sensitive ears would assume there was only one speaker."

8. **Burgundy** (p. 627) means *dark purplish-red.*

Synonyms: Select the word or phrase whose meaning is closest to the word in capital letters.

Drills

1. OBSCURE
   - A. rangy
   - B. misanthropic
   - C. recondite
   - D. egregious
   - E. opaque

2. GOAD
   - A. allay
   - B. ameliorate
   - C. conciliate
   - D. palliate
   - E. prod

3. PACIFY
   - A. propitiate
   - B. incite
   - C. spur
   - D. thwart
   - E. stymie

4. BURGUNDY
   - A. tawny
   - B. fulvous
   - C. yellowish-brown
   - D. purplish-red
   - E. in tandem

Analogies: Select the answer choice that best completes the meaning of the sentence.

5. Pacify is to goad as
   - A. appease is to acquiesce
   - B. assuage is to commend
   - C. mollify is to incite
   - D. rankle is to spur
   - E. pique is to prod

6. Misanthropic is to gregarious as
   - A. obscure is to abstruse
   - B. repentant is to contrite
   - C. heinous is to iniquitous
   - D. nebulous is to equivocal
   - E. subjective is to objective

Sentence Completions: Choose the word that, when inserted in the sentence, <u>best</u> fits the meaning of the sentence as a whole.

7. Ali was generally _____ and avoided most interactions with other people.
   - A. misanthropic
   - B. sanguine
   - C. inquisitive
   - D. clandestine
   - E. reproachful

8. Franny enjoyed _____ books that few others could understand.
   - A. burgundy
   - B. egregious
   - C. palliative
   - D. recondite
   - E. histrionic

1. **C.** *Obscure* and *recondite* mean *difficult to understand*. *Rangy* means *long and slender*, *misanthropic* means *antisocial*, *egregious* means *very bad*, and *opaque* means *solid*.

2. **E.** *Goad* and *prod* mean *provoke*. *Allay, ameliorate, conciliate,* and *palliate* mean *soothe*.

3. **A.** *Pacify* and *propitiate* mean *soothe*. *Incite* and *spur* mean *provoke*. *Thwart* and *stymie* mean *prevent*.

4. **D.** *Burgundy* means *purplish-red*. *Tawny* and *fulvous* mean *yellowish-brown*, and *in tandem* means *together*.

5. **C.** "Pacify (soothe) is the opposite of goad (provoke)."
   A. Appease (soothe) is the opposite of acquiesce (reluctantly accept) . . . no.
   B. Assuage (soothe) is the opposite of commend (praise) . . . no.
   C. Mollify (soothe) is the opposite of incite (provoke) . . . yes.
   D. Rankle (irritate) is the opposite of spur (provoke) . . . no.
   E. Pique (irritate) is the opposite of prod (provoke) . . . no.

6. **E.** "Misanthropic (antisocial) is the opposite of gregarious (friendly)."
   A. Obscure (unclear) is the opposite of abstruse (unclear) . . . no.
   B. Repentant (remorseful) is the opposite of contrite (regretful) . . . no.
   C. Heinous (wicked) is the opposite of iniquitous (wicked) . . . no.
   D. Nebulous (unclear) is the opposite of equivocal (unclear) . . . no.
   E. Subjective (personal) is the opposite of objective (factual) . . . yes.

7. **A.** "Ali was generally _antisocial_ and avoided most interactions with other people."
   Use the process of elimination. *Misanthropic* means *antisocial* and works best. *Sanguine* means *optimistic*, *inquisitive* means *curious*, *clandestine* means *secret*, and *reproachful* means *scolding*.

8. **D.** "Franny enjoyed _hard to understand_ books that few others could understand."
   Recondite means *understood by few*. *Burgundy* means *dark purplish-red*, *egregious* means *very bad*, *palliative* means *soothing*, and *histrionic* means *very dramatic*.

Sacrosanct Law?

Find each of the following words on the *Breaking Dawn* page number provided. Based on the way each word is used in the book, guess at its definition.

1. **Truncated** (p. 633) might mean _____

   _____

2. **Rectify** (p. 635) might mean _____

   _____

3. **Wanly** (p. 647) might mean _____

   _____

4. **Sonar** (p. 653) might mean _____

   _____

5. **Sacrosanct** (p. 657) might mean _____

   _____

6. **Hysteria** (p. 662) might mean _____

   _____

7. **Dilapidated** (p. 666) might mean _____

   _____

8. **Baser** (p. 666) might mean _____

   _____

Let's see how you did. Check your answers, write the exact definitions,
and reread the sentence in *Breaking Dawn* where each word appears.
Then complete the drills on the next page.

1. **Truncated** (p. 633) means *shortened*. Synonyms: abbreviated, abridged, curtailed.

2. **Rectify** (p. 635) was a synonym for *compensate* (make up for) in Group 13 and means *fix* or *make right,* which makes sense since *rectus* means *right* in Latin. *Rectus* can help you remember words like *rectitude* (moral up**right**ness) and, of course, *rectangle* (a geometric shape with four **right** angles).

3. **Wanly** (p. 647) means *weakly* or *in a strained way*. Everybody is uncomfortable; Bella is smiling **wanly** (with strain) because she is planning for Renesmee's escape without her, and Jenks is *grimacing* (frowning) because he's dealing with a vampire.

4. **Sonar** (p. 653) means *the system of using sound to locate objects in one's environment*. Interestingly, the name *sonar* comes from **SO**und **NA**vigation and **R**anging, that is, using sound to locate objects (like fish in Charlie's case) in one's environment.

5. **Sacrosanct** (p. 657) means *sacred and not to be messed with*. Synonyms: hallowed, inviolable.

6. **Hysteria** (p. 662) means *panic* or *intense emotion*. This reminds me of the great SAT and ACT word *histrionic* (very dramatic), which was a synonym for *melodramatic* in Group 15. You can see how they are related. *Panic* and *intense emotion* are *very dramatic*.

7. **Dilapidated** (p. 666) means *run-down*. This word makes me think of the "dilapidated motorcycles rusting in the Markses' front yard" that Bella found and Jacob fixed up in *New Moon*. Synonyms: decrepit, ramshackle.

8. **Baser** (p. 666) means *immoral*. Synonyms for *base*: debauched, dissolute, ignoble, iniquitous, reprobate, sordid, unscrupulous. *Iniquitous* is an interesting word to break apart. *In-* means *not* and *equi-* refers to *equal,* so *iniquitous* means *not equal—unjust*. Let's use another synonym to play *Name That Movie!* Name the movie in which James Norrington said, "Think again, Miss Swann. Vile and dissolute creatures, the lot of them." Hint: Not Bella **Swann,** but a different **Swann** in a different series of movies. (Check your answer in the Quiz and Review Solutions.)

Synonyms: Select the word or phrase whose meaning is closest to the word in capital letters.

1. TRUNCATED
   A. curtailed
   B. debauched
   C. ignoble
   D. iniquitous
   E. reprobate

2. WAN
   A. dilapidated
   B. weak
   C. decrepit
   D. ramshackle
   E. hallowed

3. SACROSANCT
   A. staid
   B. decorous
   C. omniscient
   D. inexorable
   E. inviolable

4. BASE
   A. equanimous
   B. dissolute
   C. urbane
   D. fleeting
   E. vain

Analogies: Select the answer choice that best completes the meaning of the sentence.

5. Dilapidated is to pristine as
   A. decrepit is to intact
   B. ramshackle is to sordid
   C. debauched is to truncated
   D. dissolute is to abbreviated
   E. ignoble is to curtailed

6. Rectify is to problem as
   A. bite is to vampire
   B. correct is to loam
   C. edit is to essay
   D. reanimate is to sonar
   E. truncate is to hysteria

Sentence Completions: Choose the word or words that, when inserted in the sentence, <u>best</u> fits the meaning of the sentence as a whole.

7. Ms. Darbus considered cell phones to be one of the _____ human inventions and was thrown into _____ whenever one rang in her classroom.
   A. ramshackle .. accolades
   B. sacrosanct .. histrionics
   C. wan .. rectitude
   D. obscurest .. adulation
   E. baser .. hysterics

8. Nadine considered the Beatles to be _____; she would not tolerate any negative comments about them or their music.
   A. sacrosanct
   B. inauspicious
   C. menacing
   D. serene
   E. futile

1. **A.** *Truncated* and *curtailed* mean *shortened. Debauched, ignoble, iniquitous,* and *reprobate* mean *immoral.*

2. **B.** *Wan* means *weak. Dilapidated, decrepit,* and *ramshackle* mean *run-down. Hallowed* means *sacred.*

3. **E.** *Sacrosanct* and *inviolable* mean *sacred and not to be messed with. Staid* and *decorous* mean *dull and unadventurous, omniscient* means *all-knowing,* and *inexorable* means *unstoppable.*

4. **B.** *Base* and *dissolute* mean *immoral. Equanimous* means *calm, urbane* means *stylish and charming, fleeting* means *temporary,* and *vain* means *useless.*

5. **A.** "Dilapidated (run-down) is the opposite of pristine (perfect, pure)."
   - (A.) Decrepit (run-down) is the opposite of intact (undamaged) . . . yes.
   - B. Ramshackle (run-down) is the opposite of sordid (immoral) . . . no.
   - C. Debauched (immoral) is the opposite of truncated (shortened) . . . no.
   - D. Dissolute (immoral) is the opposite of abbreviated (shortened) . . . no.
   - E. Ignoble (immoral) is the opposite of curtailed (shortened) . . . no.

6. **C.** "Rectify means fix a problem."
   - A. Bite means fix a vampire . . . no.
   - B. Correct means fix a loam (soil) . . . no.
   - (C.) Edit means fix an essay . . . yes.
   - D. Reanimate (bring back to life) means fix a sonar (sound navigation) . . . no.
   - E. Truncate (shorten) means fix a hysteria (panic) . . . no.

7. **E.** "Ms. Darbus considered cell phones to be one of the _____ human inventions and was thrown into _____ whenever one rang in her classroom."

   About once per test, the SAT gives you a sentence in which there is no evidence what words you need for the blanks. In this case, decide if the words should have similar or opposite meanings. In this question, if the first word is positive, Ms. Darbus will have a positive reaction, and if the first word is negative, so will be her response. The words in choice E fit perfectly: She thinks cell phones are a *baser* (immoral) invention and is thrown into *hysterics* (a panic) whenever one rings.

8. **A.** "Nadine considered the Beatles to be <u>not negative;</u> she would not tolerate any negative comments about them or their music."

   Sacrosanct means *sacred and not to be messed with* and fits best. *Inauspicious* means *threatening* or *unlucky. Menacing* means *threatening, serene* means *calm,* and *futile* means *useless.*

Group 35
Contraband

Find each of the following words on the *Breaking Dawn* page number provided. Based on the way each word is used in the book, guess at its definition.

1. **Obsequious** (p. 666) might mean _____

_____

2. **Cursory** (p. 668) might mean _____

_____

3. **Liaison** (p. 669) might mean _____

_____

4. **Erroneous** (p. 670) might mean _____

_____

5. **Contraband** (p. 671) might mean _____

_____

6. **Satiate** (p. 671) might mean _____

_____

7. **Déjà vu** (p. 674) might mean _____

_____

8. **Manuscript** (p. 674) might mean _____

_____

Let's see how you did. Check your answers, write the exact definitions, and reread the sentence in *Breaking Dawn* where each word appears. Then complete the drills on the next page.

1. **Obsequious** (p. 666) means *excessively obedient*. Synonyms: fawning, ingratiating, oleaginous, servile, sycophantic, toady. I've seen almost every one of these words on the SAT. Learn them and you'll gain points!

2. **Cursory** (p. 668) means *quick and not thorough*. Bella describes her "cursory glance," saying Jenks was disappointed that her "examination was **not more thorough.**" Synonyms: desultory, fleeting, hasty, perfunctory, superficial.

3. **Liaison** (p. 669) means *representative*. Jasper scares the heck out of Jenks, so he hopes Bella might take over as **representative** for the Cullens. *Liaison* has a second meaning that standardized tests sometimes use; it can also mean *a secret love affair*, which reminds me of *tryst* from Group 31. Do you think Edward ever worried that Bella was having a liaison with Jake? I suppose that Jake's thoughts would have given it away.

4. **Erroneous** (p. 670) means *incorrect* and even sounds like the word *error*. In fact, *-ous* means *characterized by*, so *erroneous* means *characterized by errors—incorrect*. Synonyms: fallacious, specious. Let's play *Name That Movie!* Name the movie and the actors who spoke the following quote: "**John Beckwith:** He lived with his mother 'til he was forty! She tried to poison his oatmeal! **Jeremy Grey:** Erroneous! Erroneous! Erroneous on both counts!" (Check your answer in the Quiz and Review Solutions.)

5. **Contraband** (p. 671) means *illegal goods*. *Contra-* means *against* and *band* refers to *ban* (a legal proclamation), so *contraband* means *against legal proclamation—illegal*.

6. **Satiate** (p. 671) means *satisfy fully*. Synonyms: sate, slake, surfeit (overfill).

7. **Déjà vu** (p. 674) refers to *the feeling of having already experienced something* and translates directly from French as *already seen*.

8. **Manuscript** (p. 674) refers to *an author's text for a book*. *Manu-* means *by hand* and *script* means *written*, so *manuscript* means *written by hand—an author's text for a book*.

146 Synonyms: Select the word or phrase whose meaning is closest to the word in capital letters.

1. OBSEQUIOUS
   A. desultory
   B. fleeting
   C. hasty
   D. sycophantic
   E. perfunctory

2. CURSORY
   A. toady
   B. hasty
   C. impassive
   D. apathetic
   E. dispassionate

3. ERRONEOUS
   A. fawning
   B. oleaginous
   C. servile
   D. sycophantic
   E. incorrect

4. SATIATE
   A. slake
   B. rectify
   C. truncate
   D. acquiesce
   E. curtail

Analogies: Select the answer choice that best completes the meaning of the sentence.

5. Obsequious is to sycophantic as
   A. fawning is to desultory
   B. oleaginous is to hasty
   C. servile is to toady
   D. sycophantic is to conditional
   E. apathetic is to zealous

6. Surfeit is to sate as
   A. inch is to mile
   B. contraband is to thief
   C. déjà vu is to matrix
   D. censure is to reproach
   E. truncate is to lengthen

Sentence Completions: Choose the word or words that, when inserted in the sentence, best fits the meaning of the sentence as a whole.

7. Though he tried to appear as a(n) _____ liaison, Wallace was actually furious to be chosen as the representative who would transport the forbidden _____.
   A. obsequious .. déjà vu
   B. erroneous .. manuscript
   C. servile .. satiety
   D. sycophantic .. contraband
   E. macabre .. taboo

8. Billy's advisor recommended that he make a careful, well thought-out decision rather than jump to a _____ conclusion.
   A. sacrosanct
   B. misanthropic
   C. recondite
   D. toady
   E. perfunctory

1. **D.** *Obsequious* and *sycophantic* mean *excessively obedient. Desultory, fleeting, hasty,* and *perfunctory* mean *quick and not thorough.*

2. **B.** *Cursory* and *hasty* mean *quick and not thorough. Toady* means *excessively obedient. Impassive, apathetic,* and *dispassionate* mean *without emotion.*

3. **E.** *Erroneous* means *incorrect. Fawning, oleaginous, servile,* and *sycophantic* mean *overly obedient.*

4. **A.** *Satiate* and *slake* mean *satisfy. Rectify* means *fix* and is the second best answer. *Rectifying* (fixing) something might *satiate* (satisfy), but *slake* (satisfy) is a much closer synonym. *Truncate* and *curtail* mean *shorten,* and *acquiesce* means *reluctantly accept.*

5. **C.** "Obsequious means sycophantic (overly obedient)."
   A. Fawning (overly obedient) means desultory (not thorough) . . . no.
   B. Oleaginous (overly obedient) means hasty (not thorough) . . . no.
   C. Servile (overly obedient) means toady (overly obedient) . . . yes.
   D. Sycophantic (overly obedient) means conditional (with reservations) . . . no.
   E. Apathetic (not caring) means zealous (passionate) . . . no.

6. **D.** "Surfeit (overfill) is more extreme than sate (satisfy)."
   A. Inch is more extreme than mile . . . no, the other way around.
   B. Contraband (illegal goods) is more extreme than thief . . . no.
   C. Déjà vu (the feeling of already having experienced something) is more extreme than matrix . . . no, "Déjà vu is . . . a glitch in the Matrix" (*The Matrix*, Warner Brothers, 1999).
   D. Censure (harsh criticism) is more extreme than reproach (less strong scolding) . . . yes.
   E. Truncate (shorten) is more extreme than lengthen . . . no.

7. **D.** "Though he tried to appear as a(n) *not furious* liaison, Wallace was actually furious to be chosen as the representative who would transport the forbidden *forbidden things*."
   Sycophantic means *overly obedient,* and *contraband* means *illegal goods,* so choice D is best.

8. **E.** "Billy's advisor recommended that he make a careful, well thought-out decision rather than jump to a *not well thought-out* conclusion."
   Perfunctory means *quick and not thorough* and fits best. *Sacrosanct* means *sacred, misanthropic* means *antisocial, recondite* means *understood by few,* and *toady* means *overly obedient.*

Quiz 7

I. Let's review some of the words that you've seen in Groups 31–35. Match each of the following words to the correct definition or synonym on the right. Then check the solutions on page 172.

1. Latent		A. Amorphous
2. Nebulous		B. Nefarious
3. Heinous		C. Pretext
4. Macabre		D. Recondite
5. Thwart		E. Abeyant
6. Pretense		F. Weak
7. Misanthropic		G. Morbid
8. Obscure		H. Stymie
9. Goad		I. Sycophantic
10. Truncate		J. Hasty
11. Wan		K. Antisocial
12. Sacrosanct		L. Prod
13. Obsequious		M. Slake
14. Cursory		N. Inviolable
15. Satiate		O. Curtail

II. Let's review several of the word parts that you've seen in Groups 31–35. Match each of the following word parts to the correct definition or synonym on the right. Then check the solutions on page 172.

16. Morph-		A. People
17. Mis-		B. Not
18. Anthrop-		C. Form
19. Rectus		D. Hate
20. In-, A-		E. By hand
21. Manu-		F. Right

Group 36

Pageantry

Find each of the following words on the *Breaking Dawn* page number provided. Based on the way each word is used in the book, guess at its definition.

1. **Pageantry** (p. 679) might mean _____

_____

2. **Cowled** (p. 679) might mean _____

_____

3. **Vindictive** (p. 680) might mean _____

_____

4. **Antithesis** (p. 681) might mean _____

_____

5. **Motley** (p. 681) might mean _____

_____

6. **Impartiality** (p. 681) might mean _____

_____

7. **Contrived** (p. 682) might mean _____

_____

8. **A wide berth** (p. 684) might mean _____

_____

Let's see how you did. Check your answers, write the exact definitions, and reread the sentence in *Breaking Dawn* where each word appears. Then complete the drills on the next page.

1. **Pageantry** (p. 679) means *organized ceremony,* like the gown competition in a beauty **pageant**—think *Miss Congeniality.* By the way, *congeniality* is a terrific SAT word meaning *pleasantness.* Synonym for *pageantry:* pomp.

2. **Cowled** (p. 679) means *hooded,* which is why the Volturi's faces are "shadowed." A *cowl* is a *large hood,* the kind you'd see a monk wearing.

3. **Vindictive** (p. 680) means *revengeful.* Synonym: vengeful.

4. **Antithesis** (p. 681) means *total opposite. Anti-* means *against* and *thesis* means *theory* or *idea,* so *antithesis* means *theory against—the total opposite.*

5. **Motley** (p. 681) means *varied.* Why is this word in the name of 1980s hard rock band Mötley Crüe? Apparently Crüe guitarist Mick Mars once heard his previous band described as "a motley looking crew." He liked the sound of it, and an American hard rock legacy was born. Apparently, the symbols (called *umlauts*) above the o and u were added just for fun. Synonyms: disparate, heterogeneous, manifold, multifarious, sundry, variegated.

6. **Impartiality** (p. 681) means *fairness. Im-* means *not,* and *partial* means *favoring,* so *impartial* means *not favoring—fair.* Synonyms for *impartial:* equitable, nonpartisan, unbiased, unprejudiced.

7. **Contrived** (p. 682) means *fake,* or more specifically *intentionally created rather than naturally occurring.* Synonyms: artificial, bogus, contrived, ersatz, fabricated, faux, feigned, inorganic, mock, spurious, synthetic.

8. **A wide berth** (p. 684) means *lots of room. Berth* is *the slot for a ship to dock in.* **A wide berth** allows the ship to dock safely without scraping the sides, just like **a wide berth** allows the Volturi witnesses to avoid bumping into the intimidating Volturi guard.

Synonyms: Select the word or phrase whose meaning is closest to the word in capital letters.

1. PAGEANTRY
   A. pomp
   B. impartiality
   C. congeniality
   D. hysteria
   E. truncation

2. MOTLEY
   A. bogus
   B. contrived
   C. fabricated
   D. heterogeneous
   E. spurious

3. IMPARTIAL
   A. disparate
   B. manifold
   C. multifarious
   D. sundry
   E. unbiased

4. CONTRIVED
   A. ersatz
   B. equitable
   C. nonpartisan
   D. unprejudiced
   E. cowled

Analogies: Select the answer choice that best completes the meaning of the sentence.

5. Ship is to berth as
   A. airport is to plane
   B. fender is to car
   C. house is to kitchen
   D. boat is to ocean
   E. car is to garage

6. Contrived is to artificial as
   A. ersatz is to feigned
   B. spurious is to unbiased
   C. motley is to congenial
   D. vindictive is to rueful
   E. cowled is to evanescent

Sentence Completions: Choose the word or words that, when inserted in the sentence, <u>best</u> fits the meaning of the sentence as a whole.

7. While Rosalie saw Jacob as the _____ of Edward, Bella saw not only their differences, but also the many similarities between the two men.
   A. pageantry
   B. vindication
   C. déjà vu
   D. pretext
   E. antithesis

8. The restaurant was known for its _____ clientele, every table filled with a heterogeneous mix of diners.
   A. sanguine
   B. amicable
   C. motley
   D. assuaged
   E. loathsome

1. **A.** *Pageantry* and *pomp* mean *organized ceremony. Impartiality* means *fairness, congeniality* means *pleasantness, hysteria* means *panic,* and *truncation* means *shortening.*

2. **D.** *Motley* and *heterogeneous* mean *varied. Bogus, contrived, fabricated,* and *spurious* mean *fake.*

3. **E.** *Impartial* and *unbiased* mean *fair. Disparate, manifold, multifarious,* and *sundry* mean *varied.*

4. **A.** Use the process of elimination. *Contrived* and *ersatz* mean *fake. Equitable, nonpartisan,* and *unprejudiced* mean *fair. Cowled* means *hooded.*

5. **E.** "A ship docks in a berth."
   A. An airport docks in a plane . . . no, the other way around.
   B. A fender docks in a car . . . no.
   C. A house docks in a kitchen . . . no.
   D. A boat docks in an ocean . . . not quite, it might sail in the ocean, but it does not dock there.
   (E.) A car docks in a garage . . . yes.

6. **A.** "Contrived means artificial (fake)."
   (A.) Ersatz (fake) means feigned (fake) . . . yes.
   B. Spurious (fake) means unbiased (fair) . . . no.
   C. Motley (varied) means congenial (pleasant) . . . no.
   D. Vindictive (revengeful) means rueful (regretful) . . . no.
   E. Cowled (hooded) means evanescent (temporary) . . . no.
   Choice A is best; it has the most direct and clear relationship.

7. **E.** "While Rosalie saw Jacob as the _opposite_ of Edward, Bella saw not only their differences, but also the many similarities between the two men."
   Antithesis means *total opposite* and fits best.

8. **C.** "The restaurant was known for its _heterogeneous_ clientele, every table filled with a heterogeneous mix of diners."
   Motley and *heterogeneous* mean *varied.* You know what *heterogeneous* means, but even if you did not, when there is a word that you don't know in the question, cross it out and try without it. Usually you don't need any one specific word to get a question correct; the SAT designs it that way. In this question, "mix of diners" also tells you that *motley* (varied) is correct. *Sanguine* means *optimistic, amicable* means *friendly, assuaged* means *soothed,* and *loathsome* means *worthy of hatred.*

Artifice

Find each of the following words on the *Breaking Dawn* page number provided. Based on the way each word is used in the book, guess at its definition.

1. **Battalion** (p. 687) might mean _____

_____

2. **Artifice** (p. 687) might mean _____

_____

3. **Apex** (p. 690) might mean _____

_____

4. **Recoil** (p. 690) might mean _____

_____

5. **Reprieve** (p. 694) might mean _____

_____

6. **Cudgel** (p. 695) might mean _____

_____

7. **Summit** (p. 695) might mean _____

_____

8. **Lilt** (p. 696) might mean _____

_____

Let's see how you did. Check your answers, write the exact definitions, and reread the sentence in *Breaking Dawn* where each word appears. Then complete the drills on the next page.

1. **Battalion** (p. 687) looks like *battle* and means *group of military troops.*

2. **Artifice** (p. 687) means *deception* or *trickery. Artificial* was a synonym for *contrived* (faked) in Group 36 and means *human-made rather than naturally occurring,* like artificial sweeteners or artificial flavors. Synonyms for *artifice:* chicanery, contrivance, duplicity, fraud, guile, spuriousness.

3. **Apex** (p. 690) means *highest point.* Synonyms: acme, apogee, peak, pinnacle, summit, zenith. A fancy word for the *lowest point* is *nadir.* At the beginning of the first *Iron Man* movie, Tony Stark is receiving the fictitious **Apogee** Award for excellence. The word *apex* and its synonyms, including **apogee,** are often used in the name of awards that honor the **highest point** of achievement in a field or pursuit.

4. **Recoil** (p. 690) means *backlash.* This word means exactly what it sounds like. Imagine a snake that's coiled up and comes forward, but then **recoils**—it backs away and winds itself back up. *Re-* means *again,* as in reapply, reborn, reclaim, and resend.

5. **Reprieve** (p. 694) means *pardon.* Synonym: amnesty.

6. **Cudgel** (p. 695) means *short, thick club.* Synonyms: bludgeon, shillelagh, truncheon. *Truncheon* reminds me of *truculent* from Group 25, which makes sense since using a *truncheon* (short club) is pretty *truculent* (hostile).

7. **Summit** (p. 695) means *meeting between heads of governments.* As you learned above, it can also mean *highest point,* as in the summit of a mountain.

8. **Lilt** (p. 696) means *rhythmically changing pitch.* Synonyms: cadence, intonation.

Synonyms: Select the word or phrase whose meaning is closest to the word in capital letters.

1. ARTIFICE
   A. recoil
   B. impartiality
   C. congeniality
   D. chicanery
   E. pageantry

2. APEX
   A. nadir
   B. battalion
   C. insouciance
   D. zenith
   E. antithesis

3. REPRIEVE
   A. amnesty
   B. bludgeon
   C. truncheon
   D. shillelagh
   E. liaison

4. LILT
   A. apathy
   B. cadence
   C. facade
   D. guise
   E. timbre

Analogies: Select the answer choice that best completes the meaning of the sentence.

5. Cudgel is to club as
   A. truncheon is to shillelagh
   B. apogee is to pinnacle
   C. reprieve is to pardon
   D. battalion is to group
   E. berth is to boat

6. Nadir is to zenith as
   A. intonation is to lilt
   B. summit is to governments
   C. verisimilitude is to belligerence
   D. deluge is to inundation
   E. desolation is to elation

Sentence Completions: Choose the word that, when inserted in the sentence, <u>best</u> fits the meaning of the sentence as a whole.

7. Emmett's arms were like two _____, intimidating vampires and humans alike with their thick muscles.
   A. catalysts
   B. polemics
   C. cudgels
   D. torrents
   E. mandates

8. Smoke from the mountain's _____ could be seen for miles and signaled to everyone nearby that the hikers had reached the top.
   A. intonation
   B. battalion
   C. duplicity
   D. summit
   E. fraud

1. **D.** *Artifice* and *chicanery* mean *trickery. Recoil* means *backlash, impartiality* means *fairness, congeniality* means *pleasantness,* and *pageantry* means *organized ceremony.*

2. **D.** *Apex* and *zenith* mean *highest point. Nadir* means *lowest point, battalion* means *group of military troops, insouciance* means *lack of caring,* and *antithesis* means *total opposite.*

3. **A.** *Reprieve* and *amnesty* mean *pardon. Bludgeon, truncheon,* and *shillelagh* mean *short, thick clubs. Liaison* means *representative.*

4. **B.** *Lilt* and *cadence* mean *rhythmically changing pitch. Apathy* means *lack of caring, facade* and *guise* mean *false display,* and *timbre* means *tone.*

5. **D.** "A cudgel is a type of club."
   - A. A truncheon is a type of shillelagh . . . no, they are both *clubs.*
   - B. An apogee is a type of pinnacle . . . no, they both mean *highest point.*
   - C. A reprieve is a type of pardon . . . no, *reprieve* means *pardon.*
   - D. A battalion is a type of group . . . yes, a *battalion* is *a type of group—a group of military troops.*
   - E. A berth is a type of boat. . . . no, a *berth* is *where a boat is docked.*

6. **E.** "Nadir (lowest point) is the opposite of zenith (highest point)."
   - A. Intonation (change in pitch) is the opposite of lilt (change in pitch) . . . no.
   - B. Summit (meeting between government heads) is the opposite of governments . . . no.
   - C. Verisimilitude (believability) is the opposite of belligerence (hostility) . . . no.
   - D. Deluge (flood) is the opposite of inundation (flood) . . . no.
   - E. Desolation (misery) is the opposite of elation (being thrilled) . . . yes.

7. **C.** "Emmett's arms were like two *????,* intimidating vampires and humans alike with their thick muscles."

   If you can't think of a word to fill the blank, try the choices and use the process of elimination. *Cudgels* means *short, thick clubs.* Emmet's arms may have been like *catalysts* (motivators), *polemics* (angry speeches), *torrents* (floods), or *mandates* (commands), but in the question you have evidence only that his arms **intimidated** and had "**thick** muscles," so *cudgels* fits best.

8. **D.** "Smoke from the mountain's *top* could be seen for miles and signaled to everyone nearby that the hikers had reached the top." *Summit* means *highest point* and fits the evidence best.

Group 38
Injudicious Accusations

Find each of the following words on the *Breaking Dawn* page number provided. Based on the way each word is used in the book, guess at its definition.

1. **Errant** (p. 699) might mean _____

   _____

2. **Contrivances** (p. 701) might mean _____

   _____

3. **Abide** (p. 702) might mean _____

   _____

4. **Infamy** (p. 702) might mean _____

   _____

5. **Impotently** (p. 702) might mean _____

   _____

6. **Specious** (p. 705) might mean _____

   _____

7. **Vexation** (p. 711) might mean _____

   _____

8. **Injudicious** (p. 712) might mean _____

   _____

158 Let's see how you did. Check your answers, write the exact definitions, and reread the sentence in *Breaking Dawn* where each word appears. Then complete the drills on the next page.

Definitions

1. **Errant** (p. 699) means *stray* and comes from the word *err,* meaning *make a mistake.* So Aro's *errant* thought was a **mistake**—his thoughts had **strayed.** I don't think Aro really considered his idea to be errant; and it's a good thing Edward can read thoughts because Aro rarely means what he says.

2. **Contrivances** (p. 701) means *schemes* or *creations.* You just learned *contrived* (fake) in Group 36. A *contrivance* (scheme) is *contrived* (fake) and used in hopes of fooling someone. Aro, Caius, and Marcus are **scheming** up reasons to attack the Cullens. Synonyms: artifice, chicanery, duplicity, gambit, guile, machinations, ruse, subterfuge.

3. **Abide** (p. 702) means *tolerate.* Synonyms: brook, countenance.

4. **Infamy** (p. 702) in this case means *obvious criminal act.* It can also mean *fame for something bad,* as in FDR's famous speech after the Japanese bombing of Pearl Harbor in which he described that day as "a date which will live in infamy." You can see the connection between the two definitions; an **obvious criminal act** would cause **fame for something bad.**

5. **Impotently** (p. 702) means *powerlessly.* You already know that *im-* means *not,* and *potent* refers to *power,* as in *omnipotent* (all powerful), so *impotent* means *not powerful—powerless.* Synonyms for *impotent:* feeble, impuissant.

6. **Specious** (p. 705) was a synonym for *erroneous* (incorrect) in Group 35 and means *misleading.* Aro and Caius are grasping for reasons to justify their attack, and Aro warns Caius against **incorrect** or **misleading** allegations (accusations). Synonyms: casuistic, fallacious, sophistic, spurious.

7. **Vexation** (p. 711) means *frustration.*

8. **Injudicious** (p. 712) means *unwise,* and *judicious* means *wise.* Synonyms: impolitic, imprudent.

Synonyms: Select the word or phrase whose meaning is closest to the word in capital letters.

1. CONTRIVANCE
   A. infamy
   B. vexation
   C. subterfuge
   D. truculence
   E. cadence

2. ABIDE
   A. countenance
   B. machinate
   C. vindicate
   D. castigate
   E. excoriate

3. IMPOTENT
   A. obsequious
   B. sycophantic
   C. toady
   D. errant
   E. impuissant

4. SPECIOUS
   A. feeble
   B. impolitic
   C. imprudent
   D. spurious
   E. pernicious

Analogies: Select the answer choice that best completes the meaning of the sentence.

5. Injudicious is to prudent as
   A. vexed is to irked
   B. impotent is to formidable
   C. transient is to ephemeral
   D. effusive is to verbose
   E. contrived is to ersatz

6. Abide is to acquiesce as
   A. tolerate is to whet
   B. countenance is to pique
   C. rankle is to palliate
   D. mollify is to presage
   E. brook is to comply

Sentence Completions: Choose the word that, when inserted in the sentence, <u>best</u> fits the meaning of the sentence as a whole.

7. Darlena was known for her _____ decisions, so classmates often asked her advice before making big changes.
   A. specious
   B. fallacious
   C. erroneous
   D. impuissant
   E. judicious

8. Mr. Kendrick was infamous within the corporation for the tricks and _____ he had used to achieve his lofty position.
   A. impotence
   B. reprieves
   C. machinations
   D. conundrums
   E. gravitas

Solutions

1. **C.** *Contrivance* and *subterfuge* mean *scheme*. *Infamy* means *fame for something bad*, *vexation* means *frustration*, *truculence* means *hostility*, and *cadence* means *rhythmically changing pitch*.

2. **A.** *Abide* and *countenance* mean *tolerate*. *Machinate* means *scheme*, *vindicate* means *get revenge for*, and *castigate* and *excoriate* mean *scold severely*.

3. **E.** *Impotent* and *impuissant* mean *powerless*. You might even recognize *impuissant* from French class as the word for *powerless*. *Obsequious, sycophantic,* and *toady* mean *overly obedient*. *Errant* means *stray*.

4. **D.** *Specious* and *spurious* mean *misleading*. *Feeble* means *weak*, *impolitic* and *imprudent* mean *unwise*, and *pernicious* means *wicked*. All of these words relate in some way to *misleading*, but *spurious* is the most direct synonym.

5. **B.** "Injudicious (unwise) is the opposite of prudent (wise)."
   A. Vexed (frustrated) is the opposite of irked (irritated) . . . no.
   (B.) Impotent (powerless) is the opposite of formidable (powerful) . . . yes.
   C. Transient (temporary) is the opposite of ephemeral (temporary) . . . no.
   D. Effusive (wordy) is the opposite of verbose (wordy) . . . no.
   E. Contrived (fake) is the opposite of ersatz (fake) . . . no.

6. **E.** "Abide (tolerate) is similar to acquiesce (reluctantly accept)."
   A. Tolerate is similar to whet (stimulate) . . . no.
   B. Countenance (tolerate) is similar to pique (stimulate) . . . no.
   C. Rankle (irritate) is similar to palliate (soothe) . . . no.
   D. Mollify (soothe) is similar to presage (predict) . . . no.
   (E.) Brook (tolerate) is similar to comply (accept) . . . yes.
   Using the process of elimination, choice E is best.

7. **E.** "Darlena was known for her _good_ decisions, so classmates often asked her advice before making big changes."
   Judicious means *wise*. *Specious* and *fallacious* mean *misleading*, *erroneous* means *incorrect*, and *impuissant* means *powerless*.

8. **C.** "Mr. Kendrick was infamous within the corporation for the tricks and _tricks_ he had used to achieve his lofty position."
   Machinations means *schemes* and best fits the evidence "tricks." *Impotence* means *powerlessness*, *reprieves* means *pardons*, *conundrums* means *riddles*, and *gravitas* means *seriousness*—none of these would necessarily make him *infamous* (famous for something bad) when used to achieve a *lofty* (high) position within the company.

Amiable Aro?

Find each of the following words on the *Breaking Dawn* page number provided. Based on the way each word is used in the book, guess at its definition.

1. **Tedium** (p. 712) might mean _____
   _____

2. **Amiable** (p. 713) might mean _____
   _____

3. **Equivocated** (p. 713) might mean _____
   _____

4. **Qualification** (p. 715) might mean _____
   _____

5. **Intrinsic** (p. 718) might mean _____
   _____

6. **Histrionics** (p. 718) might mean _____
   _____

7. **Sycophantic** (p. 719) might mean _____
   _____

8. **Chortled** (p. 727) might mean _____
   _____

Let's see how you did. Check your answers, write the exact definitions, and reread the sentence in *Breaking Dawn* where each word appears. Then complete the drills on the next page.

1. **Tedium** (p. 712) means *boredom*.

2. **Amiable** (p. 713) means *friendly*. Synonyms: affable, amicable, cordial, genial.

3. **Equivocated** (p. 713) means *used unclear language to avoid committing to an answer,* like "beating around the bush." Synonyms: circumlocuted, circumvented, eluded, evaded, prevaricated. And here's one more ridiculously high-level standardized-test word: tergiversated. Throw that one into your next essay and you'll definitely gain a point!

4. **Qualification** (p. 715) can mean *reservation* or *condition*. The SAT and ACT love to use the word *unqualified* (without reservations or conditions—total) and its synonyms *unconditional, unequivocal, unmitigated,* and *untempered*.

5. **Intrinsic** (p. 718) means *inborn* or *fundamental*. Synonyms: connate, indelible, inherent, innate.

6. **Histrionics** (p. 718) means *dramatics*. *Histrionic* was a synonym for *melodramatic* in Group 15. The other synonym was *operatic*.

7. **Sycophantic** (p. 719) means *excessively obedient and flattering to get something from someone of power,* basically a *suck-up,* which even sounds a bit like *sycophantic*. Garrett describes the word for you right before he says it, "Do you wish me to call you *master,* too, like your sycophantic guard?" A sycophantic person acts in an *obsequious, oleaginous, toady, or servile* (all four of these excellent vocab words mean *overly obedient*) way and flatters excessively to get what he or she wants.

8. **Chortled** (p. 727) basically means *chuckled* and was actually invented by Lewis Carroll in the stories of *Alice in Wonderland*. It's a mixture of the words *chuckled* and *snorted!*

Synonyms: Select the word or phrase whose meaning is closest to the word in capital letters.

1. AMIABLE
   A. tedious
   B. qualified
   C. unconditional
   D. intrinsic
   E. affable

2. EQUIVOCATE
   A. tergiversate
   B. mitigate
   C. chortle
   D. vex
   E. abide

3. HISTRIONIC
   A. amicable
   B. cordial
   C. melodramatic
   D. genial
   E. connate

4. SYCOPHANTIC
   A. acrimonious
   B. indelible
   C. inherent
   D. impolitic
   E. obsequious

Analogies: Select the answer choice that best completes the meaning of the sentence.

5. Equivocate is to prevaricate as
   A. elude is to lope
   B. circumlocute is to adore
   C. circumvent is to avoid
   D. tergiversate is to venerate
   E. temper is to absolve

6. Histrionic is to equanimous as
   A. sycophantic is to intrinsic
   B. toady is to unmitigated
   C. servile is to genial
   D. obsequious is to amiable
   E. loquacious is to terse

Sentence Completions: Choose the word that, when inserted in the sentence, <u>best</u> fits the meaning of the sentence as a whole.

7. Vaughn chortled at the obvious _____ behavior of the partygoers who were there only to gain the favor of the party's powerful host.
   A. histrionic
   B. unconditional
   C. unequivocal
   D. sycophantic
   E. petulant

8. Mr. Chen believed that it was the _____ and unconditional right of all creatures to be treated with fairness and compassion.
   A. errant
   B. impuissant
   C. affable
   D. multifarious
   E. intrinsic

1. **E.** *Amiable* and *affable* mean *friendly*. *Tedious* means *boring, qualified* means *with reservations, unconditional* means *without reservations,* and *intrinsic* means *inborn.*

2. **A.** *Equivocate* and *tergiversate* mean *use unclear language to avoid committing to an answer. Mitigate* means *lessen, chortle* means *chuckle, vex* means *frustrate,* and *abide* means *tolerate.*

3. **C.** *Histrionic* and *melodramatic* mean *very dramatic. Amicable, cordial,* and *genial* mean *friendly;* and *connate* means *inborn.*

4. **E.** *Sycophantic* and *obsequious* mean *overly obedient. Acrimonious* means *hostile, indelible* and *inherent* mean *fundamental,* and *impolitic* means *unwise.*

5. **C.** "Equivocate means prevaricate (use unclear language to avoid committing to an answer)."
   A. Elude (avoid) means lope (run) . . . no.
   B. Circumlocute (avoid) means adore . . . no.
   C. Circumvent (avoid) means avoid . . . yes.
   D. Tergiversate (avoid) means venerate (love) . . . no.
   E. Temper (lessen) means absolve (free of blame) . . . no.
   Using the process of elimination, choice C is best.

6. **E.** "Histrionic (very dramatic) is the opposite of equanimous (calm)."
   A. Sycophantic (overly obedient) is the opposite of intrinsic (inborn) . . . no.
   B. Toady (overly obedient) is the opposite of unmitigated (without reservations) . . . no.
   C. Servile (overly obedient) is the opposite of genial (friendly) . . . no.
   D. Obsequious (overly obedient) is the opposite of amiable (friendly) . . . no.
   E. Loquacious (chatty) is the opposite of terse (brief) . . . yes.

7. **D.** "Vaughn chortled at the obvious _trying to gain favor_ behavior of the partygoers who were there only to gain the favor of the party's powerful host."
   Sycophantic means *overly obedient to gain favor* and fits best. The partygoers may have been *histrionic* (very dramatic), *unconditional* (without reservations), *unequivocal* (without reservations), or even *petulant* (irritable), but you have evidence only that they were at the party "to gain the favor of the party's powerful host."

8. **E.** "Mr. Chen believed that it was the _unconditional_ and unconditional right of all creatures to be treated with fairness and compassion."
   Use the process of elimination. *Unconditional* means *without reservation,* so *intrinsic,* which means *inborn* or *fundamental,* fits best. *Errant* means *stray, impuissant* means *powerless, affable* means *friendly,* and *multifarious* means *varied.*

Group 40

Exodus

Find each of the following words on the *Breaking Dawn* page number provided. Based on the way each word is used in the book, guess at its definition.

1. **Cloying** (p. 728) might mean _____

   _____

2. **Charade** (p. 729) might mean _____

   _____

3. **Teak** (p. 733) might mean _____

   _____

4. **Benign** (p. 739) might mean _____

   _____

5. **Swagger** (p. 740) might mean _____

   _____

6. **Ardently** (p. 740) might mean _____

   _____

7. **Nomads** (p. 743) might mean _____

   _____

8. **Exodus** (p. 743) might mean _____

   _____

Let's see how you did. Check your answers, write the exact definitions, and reread the sentence in *Breaking Dawn* where each word appears. Then complete the drills on the next page.

1. **Cloying** (p. 728) means *disgustingly sweet*. Synonyms: mawkish, saccharine, treacly. I saw the word *treacly* stump nearly everyone on a recent SAT—everyone except people who recognized the connection to Harry Potter's favorite **sweet** desert, **treacle** tart.

2. **Charade** (p. 729) means *false display*, like the game **charades,** in which one player mimes a word or phrase, such as "Alan's satchel," that others try to guess. Synonyms: facade, farce, hoax, pretense, ruse, sham. You can play *Breaking Dawn* charades. Write down ten characters (such as Jane, Nahuel, Casius, Zafrina . . .) on slips of paper and drop them into a hat. Players take turns picking a slip of paper and silently imitating the character while others try to guess it.

3. **Teak** (p. 733) refers to a *type of tree that grows in Asia*. Teak lumber is **yellowish-brown.** Bella says that Nahuel's eyes "were the color of warm teak," so they are yellowish-brown. Interesting that they match the Cullens' amber eye color and not the *crimson* (deep red) of other vampires.

4. **Benign** (p. 739) means *kindly* or *harmless*. This word is used in medicine (a benign tumor is harmless, and a *malignant* tumor is *cancerous—malignant* means *harmful*), so you hear it regularly on *Scrubs, House,* and *Grey's Anatomy*. Synonym: innocuous.

5. **Swagger** (p. 740) means *arrogance*. The context defines the word, "Like all bullies, they're cowards underneath the swagger." Bullies behave **arrogantly.** Synonyms: bluster, bombast, braggadocio, bravado, hubris, machismo, superciliousness.

6. **Ardently** (p. 740) means *eagerly* or *passionately*. Synonyms: avidly, fervently, keenly, zealously.

7. **Nomads** (p. 743) means *wanderers*. Synonyms: itinerants, transients. Remember that the word *transient* was a synonym in Group 2 for *fleeting,* meaning *temporary*. That makes sense since a *transient* (nomad, wanderer) moves around and is always a *transitory* (temporary) visitor.

8. **Exodus** (p. 743), like the book in the Bible, refers to a *large departure*. All the vampire witnesses are saying *good-bye* and **departing** the Cullens' house.

Synonyms: Select the word or phrase whose meaning is closest to the word in capital letters.

1. CLOYING
   A. innocuous
   B. connate
   C. intrinsic
   D. inherent
   E. mawkish

2. BENIGN
   A. malignant
   B. kind
   C. ardent
   D. fervent
   E. keen

3. SWAGGER
   A. artifice
   B. contrivance
   C. superciliousness
   D. apogee
   E. reprieve

4. NOMAD
   A. teak
   B. transient
   C. sycophant
   D. truncheon
   E. liaison

Analogies: Select the answer choice that best completes the meaning of the sentence.

5. Cloying is to treacly as
   A. benign is to saccharine
   B. nomadic is to mawkish
   C. swaggering is to malignant
   D. eluded is to toady
   E. impotent is to impuissant

6. Swagger is to hubris as
   A. charade is to exodus
   B. facade is to teak
   C. hoax is to recoil
   D. pretense is to peripheral
   E. ruse is to sham

Sentence Completions: Choose the word that, when inserted in the sentence, best fits the meaning of the sentence as a whole.

7. Formerly a(n) _____ businesswoman, Corinne has traveled to many cities around the globe.
   A. itinerant
   B. saccharine
   C. cavalier
   D. clandestine
   E. prosaic

8. Bella was grateful that the Cullens could all stay put **and** would not be forced into a hasty _____ from Forks.
   A. bombast
   B. braggadocio
   C. exodus
   D. berth
   E. antithesis

Solutions

1. **E.** *Cloying* and *mawkish* mean *disgustingly sweet. Innocuous* means *harmless;* and *connate, intrinsic,* and *inherent* mean *inborn* or *fundamental.*

2. **B.** *Benign* means *kind. Malignant* means *harmful;* and *ardent, fervent,* and *keen* mean *passionate.*

3. **C.** *Swagger* and *superciliousness* mean *arrogance. Artifice* and *contrivance* mean *false display, apogee* means *highest point,* and *reprieve* means *pardon.*

4. **B.** *Nomad* and *transient* mean *wanderer. Teak* means *yellowish-brown wood, sycophant* means *an overly obedient and flattering person, truncheon* means *short club,* and *liaison* means *representative.*

5. **E.** "Cloying means treacly (disgustingly sweet)."
   A. Benign (kind) means saccharine (disgustingly sweet) . . . no.
   B. Nomadic (wandering) means mawkish (disgustingly sweet) . . . no.
   C. Swaggering (being arrogant) means malignant (harmful) . . . no.
   D. Eluded (avoided) means toady (overly obedient) . . . no.
   E. Impotent (powerless) means impuissant (powerless) . . . yes.

6. **E.** "Swagger (arrogance) means hubris (arrogance)."
   A. Charade (false display) means exodus (large departure) . . . no.
   B. Facade (false display) means teak (yellowish-brown wood) . . . no.
   C. Hoax (false display) means recoil (backlash) . . . no.
   D. Pretense (false display) means peripheral (at the edge) . . . no.
   E. Ruse (false display) means sham (false display) . . . yes.

7. **A.** "Formerly a(n) *traveling* businesswoman, Corinne has traveled to many cities around the globe."
   Itinerant means *wandering. Saccharine* means *disgustingly sweet, cavalier* means *overly casual, clandestine* means *secret,* and *prosaic* means *ordinary and unimaginative.*

8. **C.** "Bella was grateful that the Cullens could all stay put **and** would not be forced into a hasty *departure* from Forks."
   Exodus means *departure* and fits best. *Bombast* and *braggadocio* mean *arrogance, berth* means *dock,* and *antithesis* means *total opposite.*

Quiz 8

I. Let's review some of the words that you've seen in Groups 36–40. Match each of the following words to the correct definition or synonym on the right. Then check the solutions on page 172.

1. Motley		A. Equitable
2. Impartial		B. Chicanery
3. Contrived		C. Impuissant
4. Artifice		D. Heterogeneous
5. Apex		E. Spurious
6. Lilt		F. Affable
7. Abide		G. Prevaricated
8. Impotent		H. Mawkish
9. Injudicious		I. Apogee
10. Amiable		J. Cadence
11. Equivocated		K. Hubris
12. Sycophantic		L. Innocuous
13. Cloying		M. Countenance
14. Benign		N. Impolitic
15. Swagger		O. Obsequious

II. Let's review several of the word parts that you've seen in Groups 36–40. Match each of the following word parts to the correct definition or synonym on the right. Then check the solutions on page 172.

16. Anti-		A. Again
17. Im-		B. Power
18. Re-		C. Favoring
19. Thesis		D. Theory
20. Potent		E. Against
21. Partial		F. Not

Review

Match each group of synonyms to its general meaning. Then check the solutions on page 172.

1. Acrimony
   Animosity
   Antipathy
   Enmity
   Rancor

   A. Varied

2. Insubordination
   Insurgence
   Insurrection
   Mutiny
   Uprising

   B. Disgustingly sweet

3. Chary
   Circumspect
   Vigilant
   Wary

   C. Hostility

4. Acquiescence
   Assent
   Compliance
   Submission

   D. Worried and watchful

5. Disparate
   Eclectic
   Heterogeneous
   Manifold
   Motley
   Multifarious
   Sundry
   Variegated

   E. Reluctant acceptance

6. Cloying
   Mawkish
   Saccharine
   Treacly

   F. Rebellion

Quiz and Review Solutions

Quiz 1	Quiz 2	Quiz 3	Quiz 4	Groups 1–20 Review
1. D	1. D	1. D	1. D	1. F
2. A	2. A	2. A	2. A	2. A
3. F	3. F	3. G	3. F	3. E
4. B	4. B	4. F	4. G	4. D
5. G	5. H	5. B	5. B	5. B
6. C	6. J	6. J	6. J	6. C
7. K	7. C	7. L	7. K	
8. E	8. E	8. C	8. C	
9. J	9. K	9. E	9. M	
10. L	10. O	10. K	10. L	
11. H	11. N	11. H	11. I	
12. O	12. G	12. O	12. E	
13. N	13. I	13. N	13. H	
14. I	14. M	14. I	14. O	
15. M	15. L	15. M	15. N	
16. E	16. F	16. C	16. C	
17. D	17. E	17. A	17. A	
18. A	18. A	18. F	18. F	
19. F	19. B	19. B	19. E	
20. C	20. D	20. D	20. B	
21. B	21. C	21. E	21. D	

Answers to *Name That Movie!* quizzes *(continued on next page)*:

Group 2: *The Notebook,* New Line Cinema, 2004

Group 4: *Tropic Thunder,* Paramount Pictures, 2008

Quiz 5	Quiz 6	Quiz 7	Quiz 8	Review
1. C	1. D	1. E	1. D	1. C
2. A	2. A	2. A	2. A	2. F
3. E	3. F	3. B	3. E	3. D
4. H	4. B	4. G	4. B	4. E
5. D	5. H	5. H	5. I	5. A
6. J	6. I	6. C	6. J	6. B
7. B	7. C	7. K	7. M	
8. K	8. E	8. D	8. C	
9. F	9. L	9. L	9. N	
10. N	10. O	10. O	10. F	
11. M	11. N	11. F	11. G	
12. I	12. K	12. N	12. O	
13. O	13. J	13. I	13. H	
14. G	14. G	14. J	14. L	
15. L	15. M	15. M	15. K	
16. C	16. D	16. C	16. E	
17. F	17. F	17. D	17. F	
18. E	18. A or E	18. A	18. A	
19. D	19. A or E	19. F	19. D	
20. B	20. C	20. B	20. B	
21. A	21. B	21. E	21. C	

Answers to *Name That Movie!* quizzes:

Group 34: *Pirates of the Caribbean: The Curse of the Black Pearl,* Walt Disney Pictures, 2003

Group 35: *Wedding Crashers,* New Line Cinema, 2005; Owen Wilson and Vince Vaughn

Glossary

Abashed embarrassed

Aberration abnormality. Synonyms: *anomaly, deviation, divergence, perversion*

Abide tolerate. Synonyms: *brook, countenance*

Abomination monstrosity. Synonyms: *anathema, atrocity, bane, disgrace, horror, outrage*

Absolve declare free of blame. Synonyms: *acquit, exculpate, exonerate, pardon, vindicate*

Acquiescence reluctant acceptance. Synonyms: *assent, compliance, concession, submission*

Adoration love or worship. Synonyms: *reverence, veneration*

Adverse unfavorable

Agape wide open

Amiable friendly. Synonyms: *affable, amicable, cordial, genial*

Amorphous without shape, unclear

Anesthetize make unaware. Synonym: *sedate*

Angst anxiety. Synonyms: *disquietude, trepidation*

Anguish extreme pain or misery. Synonyms: *agony, desolation, despair, despondency, wretchedness*

Animosity hostility, hatred. Synonyms: *acrimony, antipathy, enmity, rancor*

Antagonistic hostile. Synonyms: *bellicose, belligerent, oppugnant, pugnacious, truculent*

Antipathy hostility

Antithesis total opposite

Apex highest point. Synonyms: *acme, apogee, peak, pinnacle, summit, zenith*

Ardently eagerly or passionately. Synonyms: *avidly, fervently, keenly, zealously*

Articulated clearly pronounced

Artifice deception or trickery. Synonyms: *chicanery, contrivance, duplicity, fraud, guile, spuriousness*

Atlas mythological Greek god who holds up the heavens (planets)

Aura atmosphere

Averse to opposed to

Aversion strong dislike, avoidance. Synonyms: *animosity, antipathy, disinclination, enmity*

Avidly eagerly. Synonyms: *ardently, fanatically, fervently, keenly, zealously*

Bane plague, curse

Baser immoral. Synonyms for base: *debauched, dissolute, ignoble, iniquitous, reprobate, sordid, unscrupulous*

Battalion group of military troops

Belfry bell tower

Benign kindly, harmless. Synonym: *innocuous*

Berating scolding angrily. Synonyms: *admonishing, censuring, chiding, rebuking, reprimanding, reproaching, reproofing*

Bereft without, feeling a strong sense of loss after the death of a loved one. Synonym: *sans*

Berth the slot for a ship to dock in

Blasé casual or bored. Synonyms: *apathetic, cavalier, dismissive, indifferent, insouciant, nonchalant, offhand, perfunctory, phlegmatic*

Blasphemy disrespect for sacred things. Synonyms: *desecration, execration, impiety, irreverence, profanity, sacrilege*

Bleak grim

Bodice part of a dress above the waist

Boggling staggered and astonished

Bolstered strengthened

Burgundy dark purplish-red

Capital deserving the death penalty, uppercase letters, a chief city, or money

Carnivores meat-eaters

Castigating severely scolding. Synonyms for castigate: *admonish, censure, chastise, chide, condemn, excoriate, rebuke, reprehend, reprimand, reproach, reproof*

Castoffs discards

Catalyst motivator. Synonyms: *impetus, precipitant, stimulus*

Cavalier casual or even casual to the point of being disrespectful. Synonym: *blasé (bored casualness)*

Cavernous very spacious. Synonyms: *capacious, voluminous*

Celestial heavenly. Synonym: *ethereal*

Censor edit inappropriate parts from a work of art

Censure severe criticism. Synonyms: *admonishment, castigation, condemnation, excoriation, obloquy, rebuke, reprimand, reproach, reproof, vituperation*

Chagrin embarrassment. Synonym: *mortification*

Chaos disorder. Synonyms: *anarchy, bedlam, mayhem, pandemonium, turmoil*

Charade false display.
Synonyms: *facade, farce, hoax, pretense, ruse, sham*

Chastened disciplined

Chided scolded. Synonyms: *admonished, berated, censured, rebuked, remonstrated, reprimanded, reproached, reproved*

Chortled chuckled

Circuitous round about

Circumnavigate sail around something

Circumspect cautious, watchful

Circumstantial indirect

Circumventing going around or avoiding. Synonyms: *eluding, prevaricating, equivocating*

Cloying disgustingly sweet. Synonyms: *mawkish, saccharine, treacly*

Combustible burnable. Synonyms: *flammable, ignitable, incendiary*

Commendation praise. Synonyms: *acclaim, accolade, appreciation, esteem, homage, kudos, plaudits, tribute*

Compensating making up or paying back for. Synonyms: *rectifying, redressing, indemnifying (compensating for harm or loss)*

Complement amount. Synonym: *contingent*

Complementary combining to improve each other. Synonyms: *compatible, harmonious, reciprocal*

Compulsory required. Synonyms: *mandatory, obligatory, requisite*

Comrade companion

Concave curved inward. Synonym: *recessed*

Conceive create. Synonym: *beget*

Condemn officially denounce. Synonyms: *censure, rebuke, reprove, reproach (less strong disapproval)*

Congealing coming together. Synonyms: *amalgamating, coalescing, converging, fusing, homogenizing*

Congeniality pleasantness

Contemporary modern. Synonym: *modish (modern and fashionable)*

Contraband illegal goods

Contrivances schemes or creations. Synonyms: *artifice, chicanery, duplicity, gambit, guile, machinations, ruse, subterfuge*

Contrived fake. Synonyms: *artificial, bogus, contrived, ersatz, fabricated, faux, feigned, inorganic, mock, spurious, synthetic*

Conundrum riddle, a confusing (and sometimes amusing) problem. Synonym: *quandary*

Convex curved out

Cordial friendly. Synonyms: *affable, amiable, convivial, genial*

Corresponding similar or matching. Synonyms: *analogous, commensurate, equivalent, homologous, proportional*

Cowled hooded

Crooned hummed or sung softly. Synonyms: *trilled, warbled*

Cudgel short, thick club. Synonyms: *bludgeon, shillelagh, truncheon*

Cursory quick and not thorough. Synonyms: *desultory, fleeting, hasty, perfunctory, superficial*

Debonair stylish and charming. Synonyms: *genteel, suave, urbane*

Defection abandonment. Synonyms: *apostasy, desertion, perfidy*

Déjà vu the feeling of having already experienced something

Deluge flood. Synonyms: *cascade, cataract, inundation, spate, torrent*

Dementia brain illness involving weakened reasoning, personality changes, and memory loss

Deprivation lack of

Desiccated very dry. Synonyms: *arid, dehydrated, parched, sere*

Desolation misery, emptiness. Synonyms: *anguish, despair, despondency, wretchedness*

Devout devoted. Synonyms: *ardent, fervent, keen, pious, reverent, staunch, steadfast, sworn, unwavering, wholehearted, zealous*

Diffuse spread out, wordy

Dilapidated run-down. Synonyms: *decrepit, ramshackle*

Disdainfully harshly and critically. Synonyms: *contemptuously, contumeliously, derisively, disdainfully, disparagingly, pejoratively, scathingly, scornfully, sneeringly, snidely*

Disposition way of being or character. Synonyms: *constitution, temperament*

Dubious unreliable, doubtful, or hesitant. Synonyms: *fallacious, sophistic, specious, spurious, suspect*

Eclectic from varied sources. Synonyms: *disparate, heterogeneous, manifold, motley, multifarious, sundry, variegated*

Edict formal declaration. Synonyms: *decree, fiat, mandate, proclamation*

Egregiously very badly

Empathy sharing another's feelings

Epitome perfect or highest example of. Synonyms: *paragon, quintessence*

Equable calm

Equanimous composed

Equilibrium balance

Equivocal unclear

Equivocated avoided.
Synonyms: *circumlocuted, circumvented, eluded, evaded, prevaricated, tergiversated*

Errant stray

Erroneous incorrect. Synonyms: *fallacious, specious*

Euphoric thrilled. Synonyms: *buoyant, ebullient, ecstatic, elated, exultant, jubilant, rapturous*

Eventuality possibility.
Synonym: *contingency*

Excruciating unbearable.
Synonym: *agonizing*

Exodus large departure

Expletive swear word.
Synonyms: *blasphemy, cuss, imprecation, obscenity, profanity*

Exultant thrilled. Synonyms: *buoyant, ebullient, ecstatic, elated, euphoric, exuberant, jubilant, rapturous*

Facilities abilities. Synonyms: *aptitudes, capacities, faculties, prowess*

Fanatical extremely devoted.
Synonyms: *ardent, avid, compulsive, fervent, fervid, keen, zealous*

Fathom understand, measure the depth of

Feeble very weak. Synonym: *frail*

Feral wild or ferocious.
Synonyms: *savage, undomesticated*

Ferocity hostility, bitterness, or determination

Fervent passionate. Synonyms: *ardent, avid, fanatical, fervid, keen, zealous*

Fervor passion. Synonyms: *ardor, zeal*

Fidelity trustworthiness

Figurative not literal

Filaments thin wires inside a lightbulb that glow when heated, threads

Finesse skill and grace.
Synonyms: *flair, poise*

Flabbergasted astonished.
Synonyms: *boggled, confounded, dumbfounded, staggered, stupefied*

Flagellate whip

Fleetingly temporarily.
Synonyms for fleeting: *ephemeral, evanescent, impermanent, transient*

Flog whip

Foreseen predicted. Synonym: *presaged*

Foreshadow advance warning

Forewarned warned in advance

Formidable very powerful

Furtively secretly and nervously. Synonyms: *clandestinely, covertly, surreptitiously*

Futilely uselessly or pointlessly. Synonym: *in vain*

Ghosted glided smoothly

Goad provoke or urge. Synonyms: *incite, prod, spur*

Gossamer delicate. Synonyms: *diaphanous, sheer, wispy*

Gratification enjoyment. Synonym: *indulgence*

Grave serious. Synonym: *solemn*

Gravitas seriousness of demeanor

Gravity seriousness, heavy

Gregarious outgoing and friendly. Antonym: *misanthropic (antisocial)*

Guffaws loud, hearty laughs

Haggard tired- and unhealthy looking

Haphazard unpredictable

Hapless unlucky

Hasty rushed. Synonyms: *impetuous, impulsive, rash, temerarious, unpremeditated*

Heinous wicked or worthy of hatred. Synonyms: *abhorrent, abominable, baleful, depraved, egregious, execrable, impious, iniquitous, malevolent, nefarious, odious, pernicious, reprehensible, villainous*

Herbivores plant eaters— vegetarians

Histrionics dramatics. Synonyms for histrionic: *melodramatic, operatic*

Horde mob

Hybrids mixtures. Synonyms: *amalgamations, fusions*

Hyperaware very aware

Hyperbole very exaggerated statement. Synonym: *superlative (exaggerate in a praising way)*

Hypocrisy acting in a different way than one recommends. Synonym: *cant*

Hysteria panic or intense emotion

Impartiality fairness. Synonyms for impartial: *equitable, nonpartisan, unbiased, unprejudiced*

Imperiously bossily. Synonym: *peremptory*

Implausible unbelievable

Implicitly completely, implied. Synonym: *unconditionally*

Impotently powerlessly. Synonyms for impotent: *feeble, impuissant*

Incognito undercover

Incredulous unbelieving. Synonym: *dubious*

Incubus male demon that has sex with women in their sleep, a cause of distress

Indifferent unconcerned or uncaring. Synonyms: *apathetic, blasé, cavalier, dismissive, dispassionate, impassive, insouciant, nonchalant, perfunctory*

Indignation anger or resentment about unfair treatment. Synonyms: *affront, ire, pique, umbrage, vexation*

Inevitable unavoidable Synonym: *impending, ineludible, inexorable*

Infallible never failing. Synonym: *unerring*

Infamy obvious criminal act, fame for something bad

Inferno massive fire

Infidelity unfaithfulness to a partner

Inflection change in pitch. Synonyms: *cadence, intonation, lilt, modulation, timbre*

Influx large inflow. Synonyms: *deluge, incursion, inundation, torrent*

Iniquitous wicked, unjust

Injudicious unwise. Synonyms: *impolitic, imprudent*

Innovative new and original. Synonyms: *avant-garde, groundbreaking, novel, pioneering, unprecedented*

Innuendos suggestive hints. Synonym: *insinuations*

Inquisitive curious

Intact complete and undamaged. Synonyms: *inviolate, pristine, undefiled, unimpaired, unscathed, unsullied*

Interdependent dependent on each other

Intrinsic inborn or fundamental. Synonyms: *connate, indelible, inherent, innate*

Introspective looking inward or thoughtful. Synonyms: *brooding (darkly introspective), contemplative, meditative, musing, pensive, reflective, ruminative*

Irate angry

Ire anger. Synonyms: *fury, wrath*

Judicious wise

Latent hidden or temporarily inactive. Synonyms: *abeyant, dormant, quiescent*

Legion association of lots of people or things. Synonym: *host*

Levity humor or lightness. Synonyms: *frivolity, gaiety, glee, jocularity, jollity, joviality, lightheartedness, merriment, mirth*

Liaison representative, secret love affair

Lilt rhythmically changing pitch. Synonyms: *cadence, intonation*

Loam rich soil

Loathsome repulsive or worthy of hatred

Loping running or jogging with a graceful stride

Luminary a person who "sheds light" and inspires others

Luminous radiant or shedding light

Macabre gruesome. Synonyms: *ghastly, gory, grisly, grotesque, hideous, morbid*

Malignant cancerous, harmful

Manfully with determination or bravery. Synonyms: *boldly, gallantly, intrepidly, pluckily, resolutely, valiantly*

Manuscript an author's text for a book

Medium canvas, vehicle, or instrument

Melodramatic very dramatic. Synonyms: *histrionic, operatic*

Menace threat. Synonyms: *hazard, peril*

Misanthropic antisocial. Antonym: *gregarious (outgoing and friendly)*

Mitigated lessened or soothed. Synonyms: *abated, allayed, alleviated, ameliorated, appeased, assuaged, attenuated, conciliated, mollified, pacified, palliated, placated, propitiated, tempered*

Monstrosity something large, outrageous, and unattractive

Morbid gruesome. Synonyms: *ghastly, gory, grisly, grotesque, hideous, macabre*

Morosely gloomily

Motes tiny pieces of material. Synonym: *scintillas*

Motley varied. Synonyms: *disparate, heterogeneous, manifold, multifarious, sundry, variegated*

Mutiny rebellion. Synonyms: *insubordination, insurgence, insurrection, uprising*

Nadir lowest point

Nebulous unclear. Synonyms: *ambiguous, amorphous, equivocal, imprecise, muddled, tenuous, vague*

Negligence carelessness

Newel post at the beginning or end of a stairway handrail

Nomads wanderers. Synonyms: *itinerants, transients*

Nuptials wedding

Objective factual

Obliterated totally destroyed. Synonyms: *annihilated, decimated, eradicated, expunged*

Obscure unclear or difficult to understand. Synonyms: *abstruse, recondite*

Obsequious excessively obedient. Synonyms: *fawning, ingratiating, oleaginous, servile, sycophantic, toady*

Ominous threatening. Synonyms: *foreboding, inauspicious, menacing*

Omnipotent all-powerful

Omniscient knowing everything

Omnivores meat- and vegetable-eaters

Opaque solid, unclear, not transparent (see-through), a difficult concept that is hard to grasp

Ornately in a fancy way. Synonyms: *elaborately, flamboyantly, lavishly, luxuriously, opulently*

Pacify make peaceful or soothe. Synonyms: *allay, ameliorate, appease, assuage, conciliate, mollify, palliate, placate, propitiate*

Pageantry organized ceremony. Synonym: *pomp*

Palatable acceptable, pleasant tasting

Pallid pale. Synonyms: *ashen, blanched, sallow, wan*

Pealing reverberating ringing. Synonyms for peal: *carillon, tintinnabulation trilling*

Pedigree ancestry. Synonyms: *bloodline, descent, genealogy, heritage, lineage*

Peripheral at the edge

Petulant irritable. Synonyms: *cantankerous, churlish, curmudgeonly, fractious, irascible, peevish, querulous, sullen*

Phantom ghostlike or unseen

Piquing stimulating, irritating. Synonym: *whetting*

Placating soothing. Synonyms: *abating, allaying, alleviating, ameliorating, appeasing, assuaging, conciliating, pacifying, palliating, propitiating, mitigating, mollifying, tempering*

Precedent an earlier example

Precipitous done before careful planning

Precocious mature at an early age

Prelude introduction. Synonyms: *commencement, overture, precursor*

Premeditation planning

Presage warn of something bad. Synonyms: *augur, forebode, foreshadow, foretell, portend, prophesy*

Pretense false display. Synonyms: *facade, guise, pretext, ruse*

Pretext false reason justifying an action. Synonyms: *facade, guise, pretense, ruse*

Pristine pure or perfect. Synonyms: *immaculate, intact, virgin*

Proactive acting in advance of something, rather than as a reaction after it has happened

Procreate reproduce. Synonyms: *breed, propagate*

Prodigious enormous

Prolific plentiful

Prolix too wordy

Prosaic regular and unimaginative. Synonyms: *conventional, pedestrian*

Provocation justification, deliberate irritation. Synonyms for provoke: *foment, goad, incite, prod, spur*

Proximity nearness. Synonym: *propinquity*

Purchase grip, something bought

Pusillanimous very shy

Pyre structure on which a body is cremated (burned), the heap of wood that fuels the fire

Qualification reservation, condition

Qualms doubts. Synonyms: *misgivings, reservations*

Quarantined isolated to prevent injury or spread of disease to others

Radius the thicker of the two forearm bones; in math, the length from a circle to the center of a circle

Raiment clothing

Rancid spoiled and foul. Synonyms: *fetid, mephitic, miasmic, putrid, rank*

Rangy long and slender

Rankled irritated. Synonyms: *affronted, galled, irked, piqued, vexed*

Razed destroyed. Synonyms: *annihilated, demolished, obliterated*

Reanimate revive or bring back to life

Rebuff refusal

Rebuke scold

Recoil backlash

Reconnaissance scouting or exploring

Rectify fix or make right. Synonym: *compensate*

Rectitude moral uprightness

Renegade traitorous. Synonyms: *apostate, dissident, heretical, mutinous, rebellious, treacherous, treasonous*

Repentant regretful for wrongdoing. Synonyms: *contrite, penitent, remorseful*

Reprieve pardon. Synonym: *amnesty*

Reproach scolding. Synonyms: *admonishment, censure, rebuke, reprimand, reproof*

Rescind take back. Synonym: *revoke*

Resigned accepting defeat or some other undesirable result

Resin gummy substance secreted by trees

Resolve determination. Synonyms: *grit, moxie, perseverance, pertinacity, pluck, tenacity*

Revelation surprising or dramatic announcement or realization

Reverence deep respect

Rhetoric style, versus substance

Rhetorically with no answer expected

Rueful regretful. Synonyms: *contrite, penitent, remorseful, repentant*

Sacrosanct sacred and not to be messed with. Synonyms: *hallowed, inviolable*

Sallow pale. Synonyms: *alabaster, ashen, blanched, pallid, sallow, wan*

Sanguine optimistic and cheerful, blood-red color. Synonyms: *buoyant, ebullient*

Sardonically sarcastic (disrespectfully mocking)

Satiate satisfy fully. Synonyms: *sate, slake, surfeit (overfill)*

Scornful harsh and critical. Synonyms: *contemptuous, contumelious, derisive, disdainful, disparaging, pejorative, scathing, sneering, snide*

Serene calm and peaceful. Synonyms: *equanimous, poised, tranquil*

Sideline secondary (less important) thing

Sinews tendons and ligaments

Sinuously gracefully. Synonyms for sinuous: *agile, lissome, lithe, nimble, supple*

Smug with excessive pride. Synonyms: *arrogant, bombastic, haughty, pompous, supercilious*

Solemn serious. Synonyms: *earnest, grave, sober, somber*

Solicitous concerned

Somberly seriously or gloomily. Synonyms: *dolefully, earnestly, gravely, lugubriously, soberly, solemnly*

Sonar the system of using sound to locate objects in one's environment

Soprano the highest singing voice

Specious misleading. Synonyms: *casuistic, erroneous, fallacious, sophistic, spurious*

Spectacle something interesting to look at

Stagnant still or stale. Synonyms: *dormant, lethargic, moribund, sluggish, static, stationary*

Staid dull and unadventurous. Synonyms: *decorous (proper), sedate, sober, somber*

Subjective intuitive or based on one's own ideas

Succubus female demon that has sex with men in their sleep

Sultry hot and humid

Summit meeting between heads of governments, highest point

Superlatives exaggerations (usually in a praising way). Synonym: *hyperboles (exaggerations of any kind)*

Surfeit overfill

Swagger arrogance. Synonyms: *bluster, bombast, braggadocio, bravado, hubris, machismo, superciliousness*

Sycophantic excessively obedient and flattering to get something from someone of power. Synonyms: *obsequious, oleaginous, toady, servile*

Synchronization coordination or harmony

Taboo something forbidden

Tactile relating to the sense of touch

Talisman magical lucky charm. Synonyms: *amulet, fetish, juju, totem*

In tandem together

In tatters in shreds. Synonym: *threadbare*

Taut tight or tense

Tawny yellowish-brown. Synonym: *fulvous*

Teak tree that grows in Asia with yellowish-brown wood

Tedium boredom

Tenor tone, highest male singing voice. Synonym: *timbre*

Tenuous weak or flimsy

Tersely briefly. Synonyms (which imply briefly, but also rudely): *brusquely, curtly, laconically*

Theatrically very dramatically

Thesis theory or idea

Thwarted prevented or blocked. Synonyms: *foiled, forestalled, stonewalled, stymied*

Timbre tone or sound quality. Synonym: *tenor*

Tirade angry and attacking speech. Synonyms: *broadside, diatribe, fulmination, harangue, invective, onslaught, philippic, polemic, rant*

Torrent flood. Synonyms: *cascade, cataract, deluge, inundation, spate*

Transient temporary, nomad or wanderer

Trepidation fear. Synonyms: *angst, foreboding*

Trilling soft and vibrating. Synonyms: *crooning, quavering, warbling*

Truncated shortened. Synonyms: *abbreviated, curtailed*

Trysts romantic encounters

Unconditionally completely—without conditions. Synonyms: *consummately, unequivocally, unqualifiedly*

Undermined weakened

Unobtrusively discreetly. Synonyms: *circumspectly, inconspicuously*

Unprecedented unheard of before

Unqualified without reservations or conditions, total. Synonyms: *unconditional, unequivocal, unmitigated, untempered*

Venomous very hostile or harmful. Synonyms: *baleful, loathsome, maleficent, malevolent, malicious, odious, rancorous*

Veracity truthfulness

Verbose wordy. Synonyms: *circumlocutory, digressive, discursive, effusive, garrulous, loquacious, periphrastic, prolix*

Verdict ruling or judgment. Synonym: *adjudication*

Verifiable confirmable

Verisimilitude the appearance of seeming true

Verity a fundamental truth

Vertigo dizziness

Vexation frustration

Vicariously through someone else

Vindictive revengeful. Synonym: *vengeful*

Viscous thick and gooey. Synonyms: *gelatinous, glutinous, mucilaginous, treacly*

Vituperative very malicious (mean) condemnation

Vocabulary list of words. Synonyms: *lexicon, lexis*

Vortex whirlpool. Synonyms: *eddy, maelstrom*

Voyeuristic deriving enjoyment from watching others

Wanly weakly, in a strained way

Ward dependent, department, district, lookout

Wary worried and watchful. Synonyms: *chary, circumspect, vigilant*

Wide berth lots of room

Yoga Indian physical and spiritual exercises aimed at achieving enlightenment

The most sensational way for students to unlock their vocabulary potential.

978-0-470-50743-8

978-0-470-53299-7

978-0-470-59696-8

978-0-470-63999-3

Now students can use these workbooks side-by-side with their own copies of Stephenie Meyer's *Twilight* saga to unlock their vocabulary potential for the *SAT, ACT®, GED®, and SSAT® exams!

WILEY
Now you know.